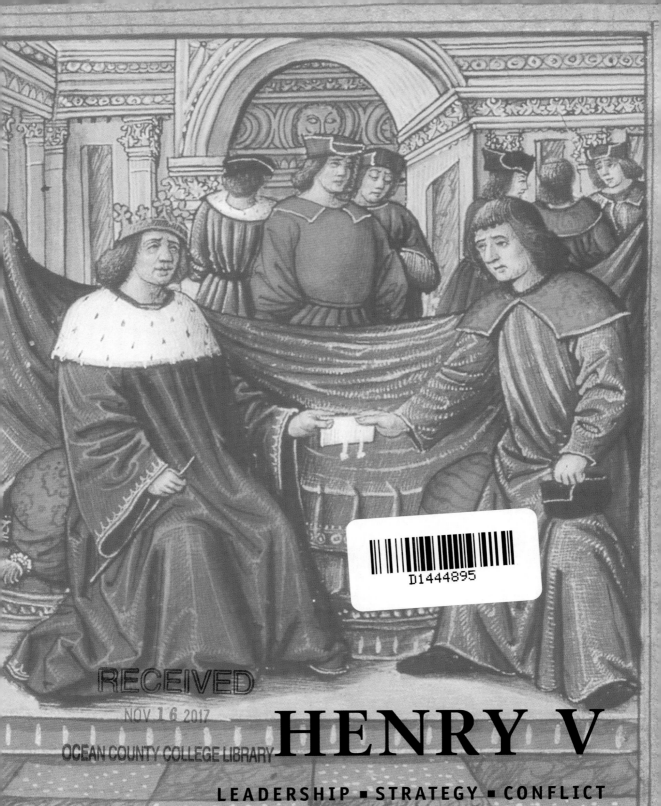

HENRY V

LEADERSHIP ■ STRATEGY ■ CONFLICT

MARCUS COWPER ■ ILLUSTRATED BY GRAHAM TURNER

First published in 2010 by Osprey Publishing
Midland House, West Way, Botley, Oxford OX2 0PH, UK
44-02 23rd St, Suite 219, Long Island City, NY 11101, USA

E-mail: info@ospreypublishing.com

ISBN: 978 1 84908 370 6
E-book ISBN: 978 1 84908 371 3

Editorial by Ilios Publishing Ltd, Oxford, UK
www.iliospublishing.co.uk
Cartography by Mapping Specialists Ltd
Page layout by Myriam Bell Design, France
Index by Alison Worthington
Originated by PPS Grasmere Ltd
Printed in China through Worldprint Ltd

10 11 12 13 14   10 9 8 7 6 5 4 3 2 1

A CIP catalogue record for this book is available from the British Library.

Dedication

For my mother Judy.

Acknowledgements

I would like to thank the following people and institutions for their
help in obtaining images for this book: Richard and Gillian Long;
Christine Reynolds, Assistant Keeper of Muniments at Westminster
Abbey; akg-images; Bridgeman Art Library.

I would also like to thank Graham Turner for his expertise in creating
the three artwork plates that adorn this title, and Don Larson and his
team at Mapping Specialists Ltd for putting together the maps.

Finally I would like to thank my wife Jo, as ever, for all her help and
support on this book.

Artist's note

Readers may care to note that the original paintings from which the
colour plates in this book were prepared are available for private sale.
The Publishers retain all reproduction copyright whatsoever.
All enquiries should be addressed to:

Graham Turner, PO Box 88, Chesham, Buckinghamshire

The Publishers regret that they can enter into no correspondence upon
this matter.

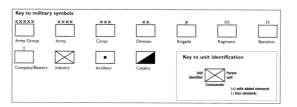

CONTENTS

INTRODUCTION

The great helm from the tomb of Henry V in Westminster Abbey. The helm forms part of a set of funeral 'achievements' of Henry V and was positioned on a wooden beam above his tomb, which was finished in 1431. The helm is of the tilting style, used for jousting. (Copyright Dean and Chapter of Westminster)

The battle of Agincourt is a prominent part of the English national myth. Immortalized in Shakespeare's *Henry V* it has been a national rallying point over the centuries, while its victor, Henry V, has been widely claimed as the greatest medieval monarch, the very epitome of medieval kingship. His military successes in France, built upon his experiences in suppressing the Welsh and aristocratic revolts of his father's reign, show him to be a military commander of the first order, well skilled in the tactics, strategies and logistical and personal skills required by a medieval commander to undertake a war of conquest. His reputation as a king was acknowledged by his contemporaries, both in England and throughout Europe, and it is a reputation that has survived through to the present day largely intact.

The unassailable Henry as shown by Shakespeare is not the true historical reality. Henry's grip on the throne of England, let alone France, was not secure in 1413. His father had usurped the rightful king, Richard II, in 1399 and been forced to deal with numerous uprisings against his rule during the first decade of the 15th century. Henry too had to deal with both popular and aristocratic upbringings until his conquests made his position secure.

These conquests in France from 1415 up to his death in 1422 were concerned with reclaiming what he saw as his lost inheritance, the Angevin lands in France that had been held by the monarchs of England in their subsidiary roles as great magnates of France. The Duchy of Normandy formed the oldest part of this inheritance, as William the Conqueror was Duke of Normandy before becoming King of England following the Norman Conquest in 1066. The marriage of Henry II to Eleanor of Aquitaine brought the enormous possessions of the Duchy of Aquitaine into the hands of the English monarchy, and at its largest extent the Angevin Empire covered almost all of Western France with the exception of Brittany – Normandy, Aquitaine, Anjou, Maine, Touraine and Poitou. The vast majority of these territories were lost during the conflict between King John of England and Philip II of France at the end of the 12th and

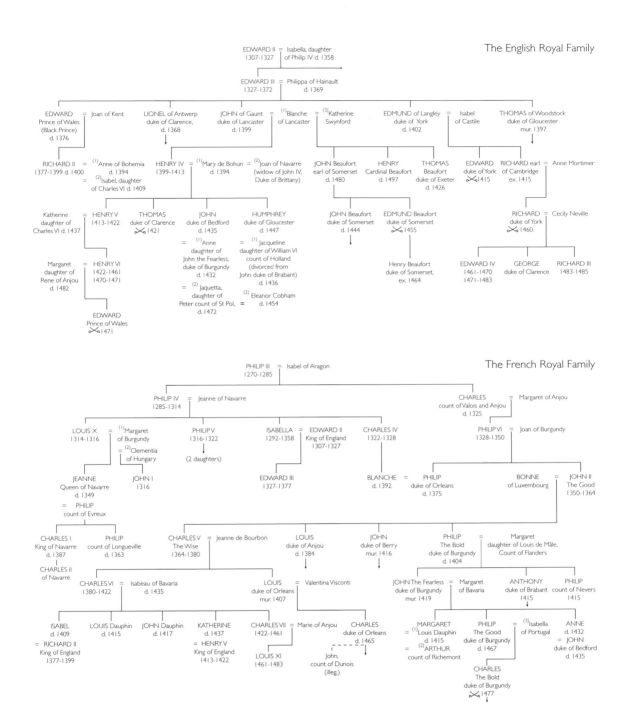

The English Royal Family

The French Royal Family

beginning of the 13th centuries, with Normandy lost by 1204. The only territory in France left to the English king was the Duchy of Aquitaine, also known as Gascony or Guienne, based around the port of Bordeaux.

This reduced territory still had the power to cause international conflict as it highlighted the duality of the King of England's position, as a sovereign in his own country but also a vassal of the King of France in his role as Duke of Aquitaine. Whenever either the king of England or France changed, the King of England was required to pay homage to the King of France for his French territories, something confirmed by the Treaty of Paris in 1259 between Henry III and Louis IX when the English king surrendered his rights to the lost territories in return for confirmation of the Duchy of Aquitaine. The King of England therefore paid homage for his French territories in 1273, 1285, 1303, 1308, 1320 and 1325, though conflict also broke out over the issue in 1294 and 1324 following French confiscation of the duchy during periods of feudal conflict. In 1337 conflict broke out once more and Philip VI of France declared that Edward III was a disobedient vassal and confiscated the duchy. However, this time the English response was different – Edward III claimed the throne of France through his grandfather, Philip IV, launching the Hundred Years War. It was this claim that Henry V would use to legitimize his programme of conquest in Normandy, and he was the closest of all the English monarchs to achieving the realization of that claim through the Treaty of Troyes of 1420 that disinherited the Dauphin and made Henry the heir to the throne of France.

Prior to this the English monarchy had used the claim to the throne of France more as a bargaining piece to extend their territorial claims, and Edward III was willing to drop using the title following the Treaty of Brétigny, which came out of the English victories at Crécy (1346) and Poitiers (1356) – the latter of which had seen the capture of the French king John II.

This treaty gave Edward III Aquitaine, Poitou, Ponthieu and the newly captured territory around Calais in full sovereignty in return for an abandonment of the English claims to the French throne, Normandy, Anjou and Maine. However, this treaty rapidly broke down and war was resumed in 1369. Henry's claims and campaigns can be seen, at least initially, as being part of this process. However, the scale of his successes and the divided nature of the French leadership – particularly following the murder of John the Fearless of Normandy in 1419 – gave him the opportunity to push further than any English king before him and make the dual monarchy of France and England a reality.

The Dunstable Swan Jewel was found during excavations at the Dominican Friary in Dunstable in 1965. It is made of white enamel on gold and dates from around the year 1400. The swan was adopted as a symbol by the house of Lancaster, and as a livery badge is particularly associated with Henry V. (British Museum, London, UK/The Bridgeman Art Library)

THE EARLY YEARS

The future Henry V was not born a royal prince, but the son of a major magnate – Henry Bolingbroke, Earl of Derby and Northampton, himself the son of John of Gaunt, Duke of Lancaster, and son of Edward III, thus making Bolingbroke first cousin of the King of England, Richard II. Henry's mother was Mary Bohun, through whom Bolingbroke obtained the Earldom of Hereford.

Henry was born in the gatehouse of Monmouth Castle in Wales on 16 September 1386, and was known in his early years as Henry of Monmouth accordingly. His mother died in 1394 at the age of 24, but not before she had given Bolingbroke three more sons, who would later become Thomas, Duke of Clarence, John, Duke of Bedford, and Humphrey, Duke of Gloucester.

Henry of Monmouth's childhood was no doubt conventional enough, though few details remain of his early years. He was certainly instructed in the military skills suitable for his class – as well as the aristocratic pursuits of hunting and falconry. Owing to his father's influence, he was unusually learned, becoming proficient in Latin, French and English under the tutelage of his uncle, Henry Beaufort. The Beauforts were the legitimized children of John of Gaunt and Katherine Swynford, and would prove influential throughout Henry's reign. There is a legend that Henry studied at Queen's College, Oxford, when Henry Beaufort was chancellor of Oxford in 1397–98 – but there is no concrete evidence of this, and the fact that he was only 10 years old at the time militates against it.

The year 1398 saw Henry's life thrown into chaos when his father was exiled following a dispute with Thomas Mowbray, Duke of Norfolk. The origins of this dispute date back to a confrontation between Richard II and some of his magnates in 1388. Henry Bolingbroke had been on the side of the magnates and had defeated the Ricardian forces at the short-lived battle of Radcot Bridge. Richard had been compelled to assent to impeachment and execution of some of his favourites in the 'Merciless Parliament' of the same year, and ever since had sought to revenge himself upon the lords who had infringed his prerogatives. In 1397 three of the five great lords who had opposed him were tried and executed or exiled, which left only Mowbray and Bolingbroke. Richard took the opportunity of the confrontation between the two of them to get rid of the last of his enemies

The young Henry of Monmouth is knighted by King Richard II during the campaign against Ireland in 1399. Henry was taken into Richard's court as a hostage following his father's banishment, and accompanied Richard during his campaign to Ireland later in the year. This illustration is taken from an early 15th-century French illuminated manuscript, the *Histoire du Roy d'Angleterre Richard II* (Ms.Harley 1319, fol.5), held in the British Library, London. (akg-images/ British Library)

and, having originally decided that the dispute between Mowbray and Bolingbroke should be settled by a judicial duel, he called it off at the last moment and banished both of them – Mowbray for life and Bolingbroke for ten years. Bolingbroke's eldest son, the young Henry of Monmouth, was taken into the king's household as a virtual hostage.

In February 1399, Bolingbroke's father, John of Gaunt, died leaving him to inherit the vast wealth and territory of the Duchy of Lancaster. However, Richard II had other ideas and in March he extended Bolingbroke's period of banishment to life and confiscated all his estates

and his inheritance. He then undertook an expedition to Ireland, taking Henry of Monmouth and his uncle, Henry Beaufort, with him. While Richard was attempting to bring the rebellious Irish to heel, Bolingbroke returned to England with a small retinue on 4 July 1399, ostensibly to claim his Duchy of Lancaster. The Earls of Northumberland and Westmorland, along with other northern magnates, rapidly joined him. Hearing the news in Ireland, Richard is supposed to have said to the young Henry of Monmouth: 'Henry, my boy, see what thy father hath done to me! He hath invaded my land and put my subjects to death without mercy, through these unhappy doings thou wilt perchance lose thine inheritance.'

While Richard delayed his return from Ireland, Bolingbroke's party gathered strength, and by the time Richard returned in early August he had very little support left. Around 10 August, Richard surrendered to Northumberland and Thomas Arundel, later Archbishop of Canterbury, at Conway Castle and was escorted to Chester as a prisoner. From this point onwards events moved rapidly. Richard was escorted to London where, on 29 September, he resigned the throne, presumably under some duress. On 30 September Parliament assembled and renounced homage and fealty to Richard, and Henry Bolingbroke claimed the throne of England through his line of descent from Henry III. He was acknowledged as Henry IV of England and his eldest son, Henry of Monmouth, was acclaimed as his heir.

On 15 October Henry, who had by now been brought back from Ireland, was granted the titles once held by the Black Prince: Prince of Wales, Duke of Cornwall and Earl of Chester; he was also made Duke of Lancaster on 10 November 1399. His cousin, the deposed King Richard, was taken as a prisoner to Pontefract Castle, where he would end his days in February 1400.

As heir to the throne of England the 13-year-old Henry's position and expectations had been transformed. He was now one of the most important figures in the country and, militarily, was required to assist his father in the establishment of the new, Lancastrian dynasty.

THE MILITARY LIFE

The first parliament of Henry IV's reign in 1399 had seen incursions by the Scots into northern England – no doubt taking advantage of the absence of the Earls of Northumberland and Westmorland, who were at Westminster – while Robert III of Scotland refused to recognize Henry IV's assumption of the throne, as did Charles VI of France. Henry therefore announced on 10 November 1399 his intention to lead an army against the Scots in the first military operation of his reign. His eldest son would go with him.

The expedition set off in May 1400 and would prove to be the future Henry V's first military experience. A large army of over 13,000 men was assembled and the army crossed the border into Scotland on 14 August. The expedition proved to be inconclusive, as Robert III withdrew in the face of the English

The campaigns of Henry V

advance while Edinburgh Castle was strongly garrisoned and, having been misled by Scottish negotiators, Henry IV withdrew from Scotland at the end of August having exhausted his supplies and achieving very little. By this stage a new threat had arisen in Wales with the revolt of Owen Glendower. This Welsh lord (see pp.49–50) had declared himself the true Prince of Wales on 16 September 1400, before sacking the nearby town of Ruthin and other towns and centres in the region. The initial impetus of the revolt was slowed when Glendower was defeated near Welshpool on 24 September. On their return from Scotland, Henry IV and Prince Henry led an expedition into Wales, though it only lasted for a week or so and failed to bring Glendower to battle.

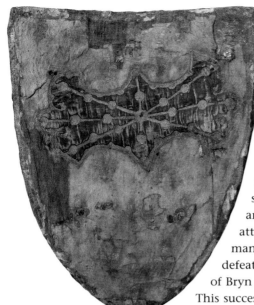

This shield is part of the military equipment associated with the tomb of Henry V. It is made of limewood and has an arm pad of crimson velvet. Scraps of the original blue silk brocade are still visible. (Copyright Dean and Chapter of Westminster)

Prince Henry was left at Chester to deal with the problem in his own principality; owing to his youth he was given a council to assist him, at the head of which was the son of the Earl of Northumberland, Henry Hotspur. The revolt stretched on into 1401, with Conwy Castle falling to a *coup de main* in that year, though it was rapidly back in English hands. Henry IV led an expedition to southern Wales in October in support of his son. This short campaign, lasting only two weeks, took in Llandovery and the monastery at Strata Florida, but again failed to achieve anything substantial, and Glendower felt bold enough to launch an assault on Caernarvon Castle shortly afterwards and attack Welshpool once more. In April 1402 Glendower managed to capture Lord Grey of Ruthin, while on 22 June he defeated an army led by Sir Edmund Mortimer at the battle of Bryn Glas, capturing him and killing some 1,100 of his men. This success, followed up by Glendower's assaults on the towns of Abergavenny, Caerleon, Usk, Newport and Cardiff in southern Wales led to Henry IV undertaking another punitive expedition in September 1402, dividing his large force – chroniclers claim some 100,000 men, though this is an extreme exaggeration – into three columns, with the northernmost one commanded by Prince Henry. However, this two-week campaign was the most unsuccessful one so far, achieving almost nothing in the face of Welsh withdrawals and terrible weather conditions.

In March 1403 Henry formally became the king's lieutenant of the marches in Wales based in Shrewsbury, taking absolute command of operations against Glendower for the first time, but it was not to be in Wales that he was to face his first major battle.

The battle of Shrewsbury

The powerful Percy family of northern England – holders of many of the royal positions along the border – had become increasingly estranged from the new Lancastrian regime ever since their support had helped Henry IV win the throne in 1399. Now they decide to take matters into their own hands and allied themselves with Glendower, whose prisoner (and Henry Hotspur's brother-in-law) Sir Edmund Mortimer had married his daughter and gone over to his side. They sought to overthrow the Lancastrian rule and replace Henry IV with the young Earl of March, Mortimer and Hotspur's nephew, who in many ways had a superior claim to the throne of England than Henry IV (see the family tree on p.5).

The rebels' plan was that Hotspur, along with his uncle the Earl of Worcester, would march from Chester to Shrewsbury both to meet up with Glendower's forces moving northwards and to capture Prince Henry who was based there. At the same time his father, the Earl of Northumberland, would gather another force in the north.

Henry IV, who was already travelling northwards, had certainly found out about the conspiracy by 12 July and, assembling what men he could, he marched for Shrewsbury on 17 July, arriving there before Hotspur and linking up with his 16-year-old son.

Henry Hotspur arrived with his force on the 20th and, as Glendower and Northumberland were both delayed, found himself caught between the fortified town of Shrewsbury and the bulk of the royal forces. He withdrew 3 miles (5km) to the north-west to the village of Berwick and prepared to give battle.

The two armies appear to have been roughly of an equal size, though the exact numbers involved are unknown. Anything from as low as 5,000 men to the figure of 14,000 given in the *Annales Henrici Quarti* seems plausible – though contemporary chroniclers again give widely varying totals of anything up to 80,000. The forces on both sides consisted of a mixture of men-at-arms and archers, with a detachment of Cheshire archers on the Percy side proving to be particularly influential in the course of the battle.

Hotspur had drawn his men up in a line of battle on a low hill in Berwick Field at the top of a field of peas. Henry IV split his army into two main divisions, described as follows by the French chronicler Jean de Waurin:

> The king... made his dispositions of vanguard, main body, and rear guard, of whom he delivered the command to those whom he thought proper and worthy to undertake it. He in person led the main body, the Duke of York, his uncle, being with him, and the young Duke of Gloucester, the Earl of Arundel, the Earl of Rutland, and many other great lords. In the vanguard were the Earl of Warwick, the Earl of Exeter, the Earl of Somerset, the Lord de Ros, and many other great barons, and in the rear guard were the young Duke of Surrey and many wise and distinguished knights, and when they were all assembled they numbered fully twenty-six thousand archers and three thousand men-at-arms, but at last there were more than sixty thousand men.

Prince Henry commanded a third force to the flank of the main army. There then followed a period of negotiations between the two sides, during which the Percys rejected extremely good terms from Henry IV. The battle itself started in the afternoon with the advance of the Royal vanguard under Edmund, Earl of Stafford, who had just been appointed constable of England by Henry. His force advanced uphill into the face of the Percys' force of Cheshire archers and took heavy casualties. The *Chronica Maiora* of Thomas Walsingham describes it as follows: 'Therefore the archers of Henry Percy began the fight and the place for the missiles was not on the ground... for men fell on the king's side as fast as leaves fall in autumn after the hoar-frost. Nor did the king's archers fail to do their work, but sent a shower of sharp points against their adversaries.'

Despite the arrow storm, Stafford's men came face to face with the Percy line and were driven back, with the Earl of Stafford being killed in the process. At this point, Henry IV led his main force forwards up the hill, while at the same time summoning his son to attack the Percy flank.

The sword of Henry V from Westminster Abbey. This arming sword was found in the Triforium of Westminster Abbey in 1869 and, although located separately, is believed to be one of the funeral 'achievements' of Henry V. (Copyright Dean and Chapter of Westminster)

With his men being overwhelmed by the Royal force, Hotspur decided on a bold strike, launching a mounted charge of 30 men to strike straight into the enemy and kill the leaders – most importantly the king:

> Thenne was there a strong and an hard bataille, and meny were slayn on bothe sides: and whanne sere Henry Percy saw his men faste slayn he pressid in to the bataille with xxx men, and made a lane in the myddille of the ost til he cam to the kyngis baner, and there he slow the erl of Stafford and ser Thomas Blount and othir: and atte laste he was beset aboute and slayne, and anon his ost was disparblid and fledde.

English Chronicle

Hotspur's attempt had failed. Although he had killed the royal standard-bearer, Sir Walter Blount – who may well have been wearing a spare set of Henry IV's armour – he himself had fallen and his force now broke apart under pressure from Henry IV in the centre and Prince Henry on the flank.

In the course of this action, Prince Henry himself was severely wounded in the face by an arrow, as described by his biographer in *The First English Life of Henry V*:

> Wherein the courage and strength of the younge Prince Henrie appeared maruelouslie excellent; for in the same bataille, as he with a feruent mynde fought (peraduenture unwarelie) amongst the rebbeles, he was wounded in the face wth an arrowe, so sore that they that they present wth him were in despaire of his life, wherefore they pained them to with drawe him from the bataille. But that noble Prince, perceauinge theire intent gaue to them this aunswere: 'With what stomacke,' saide he, 'shall our people fight, when they see me theire Prince and the Kings sonn withdrawe my selfe, and recoile for feare. Bringe me therefore wounded as I ame amongst the first and the formost of our partie, that not only by words but also by deeds I may enforce the courage of our men, as it becommeth a Prince for to doe.

This was a major wound and it took the king's surgeon, John Bradmore, to cure it through devising a patent machine for extracting the arrowhead and then a 20-day course of ointments and cleansing to ensure that the prince did not die of any post-operative infection. However, it must have left a major scar and been a permanent reminder to the prince of the power and effect of massed archers on the battlefield.

The battle itself could have caused as many as 5,000 casualties. Adam of Usk places the number much higher in his chronicle: 'This battle saw terrible slaughter on both sides, leading to the loss of sixteen thousand lives, but in the end it was the king who, having begun the assault, emerged as the victor. Sad to say, this Sir Henry, the flower and glory of Christian knighthood, died in the battle, as did his afore-mentioned uncle…'

The Earl of Worcester was not killed in the battle itself, but executed two days later along with a number of other notable leaders of the revolt. The body of Hotspur his nephew was displayed in Shrewsbury before being quartered and distributed throughout the kingdom. His head was displayed in York, looking out over his lands. Henry IV also moved swiftly to isolate the Earl of Northumberland, who lost a number of his offices and titles and was held in custody for a period.

While the revolt of the Percy family had been crushed for now, the problem of Owen Glendower remained. Prince Henry was to spend much of the next decade subduing the revolt and securing his principality.

The Welsh campaigns

Glendower had been prevented from joining up with his allies at Shrewsbury, but his revolt was far from over. Throughout 1403 it gathered momentum and took on a new severity. Henry IV took action, as *The First English Life of Henry V* records: 'And for because they perceived in theire obstinacie the Kinge deliuered the Prince, his Sonn, a greate armed bande, and sent him into Wales to subdue those falsh Welsh rebellions, who, at his comminge into Wales, destroyed theire lande wth sworde and fyre.'

In 1404 the rebels struck their most serious blow yet, when they captured the towns and castles of Harlech and Aberystwyth, with Glendower using the former as his residence and the latter as his administrative centre. Later in the year the town of Kidwelly was also captured and burned, allegedly with assistance from a French fleet.

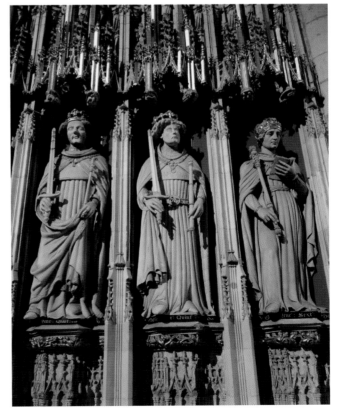

The ornately carved Quire Screen in York Minster contains sculptures of all English kings from William the Conqueror through to Henry VI. Henry is shown here with a forked goatee beard, while he is described as being clean-shaven in his younger days.
(Richard and Gillian Long)

In 1405 the English under Prince Henry began to fight back effectively, with a force under Lord Talbot defeating Glendower's men at Grosmount in March. This was followed up by another English victory at Pwll Melyn in May that not only saw the Welsh defeated, but also the death of Glendower's brother and the capture of his eldest son, Gruffydd, who was confined in the Tower of London. Later that same year a French force under Jean de Reieux landed at Milford Haven to support Glendower's rebellion, and they attacked and burned the towns of Haverford West, Tenby and Carmarthen before marching eastwards towards England. They halted outside Worcester, where Henry IV was based, and an eight-day standoff ensured until the Franco-Welsh forces withdrew, being short of supplies.

This was the last major French intervention in the Welsh revolt, and from 1406 onwards Prince Henry was able to roll back the Welsh from the ground they had occupied the previous year. April 1406 saw a heavy defeat for Glendower's forces, while the recapture of Anglesey by English forces shipped over from Ireland cut off a major source of supplies for the rebels.

By the summer of 1407 Prince Henry felt in a strong enough position to put Aberystwyth, one of Glendower's remaining strongholds, under siege. Assembling some 600 men-at-arms and 1,800 archers, and well supplied with cannon, the siege dragged on for over a year until the castle surrendered in the autumn, as described by *The First English Life of Henry V*:

> How so be a greate part of them, seeinge their confederates thus vanquished, and themselues thus oppressed by the Prince, fledd foe refuge into a greate and stronge Castle in Wales called Amberrstmch [Aberystwyth], wherevnto the Prince layed his siege, and assaulted it by mynes and all manner of engines that were thought needful for the distruccion of them and of there Castle; he made manie vigorous assaults and skirmishes for the oppression of them. And on his partie the Siege was not wthout the paine and disease of the Prince and his companie, in so much the more noyous vnto them that were lodged wthin the Castell, not in plaine fields but in roughe and thicke woods, for wth such manner woods and Castells it was environed. And also it was that time winter, wch was cause to them of incredible colde and paine. Neuertheless this most virtuous Prince, not wearied wth paine, after he had longe assieged this castell to the Kings greate cost and expences, and not wthout the effusion of much bloud, obtained the Castell, and subdued the residue of Wales vnder the Kings obeysance.

The fall of Harlech to the prince in March 1409 left the Welsh Revolt largely subdued. Though Glendower would remain at large and isolated guerrilla attacks still occurred throughout the principality, no major centres of resistance remained and Prince Henry felt free to turn his attention towards England and the growing issues over intervention in France. One benefit of Henry's years of campaigning in Wales was that he had built up his own retinue, consisting of men such as Thomas, Earl of Arundel, and Richard, Earl of Warwick, who would serve him well in his later campaigns in France.

Plans for France

From the year 1409 Prince Henry became increasingly influential in the affairs of state as part of his role on the king's council. This was partly owing to the increased disability of Henry IV, who removed himself from a lot of the day-to-day business of running the kingdom, and partly owing to Prince Henry's increased political maturity. As he had developed a military retinue, so he now surrounded himself with a political faction, based largely around his Beaufort uncles – Henry, Bishop of Winchester, John, Earl of Somerset, and Thomas, Earl of Dorset. This faction gained power in the royal council at the expense of the established chancellor, Archbishop Arundel, and the treasurer, Sir John Tiptoft. The two opposing groups had very different attitudes to the situation in France.

The state of political affairs in France had become particularly poisonous following the murder of Louis of Orléans by John the Fearless, Duke of Burgundy, in November 1407, This solidified factions that had been developing in the French court into two groups – the Burgundians and the Armagnacs, named after Bernard, Count of Armagnac. The country was slipping into a state of near civil war and both sides sought English military support in their struggles.

Henry and his advisors sought to ally themselves with the Burgundians in 1410–11, sending an expedition under the Earl of Arundel that fought alongside the Burgundians at the battle of Saint-Cloud in October 1411. However, in November of the same year Henry IV recovered and Prince Henry and his faction found themselves out of favour at court and the English position on France was reversed, with Henry IV and his council signing the Treaty of Bourges with the Armagnacs in May 1412. This was followed up by an expedition to Gascony led by Prince Henry's younger brother, Thomas of Lancaster (now created Duke of Clarence and named the king's lieutenant in Aquitaine) in August. However, this military effort proved short lived as the Burgundians and the Armagnacs patched up their differences, leaving Thomas with no allies in France and instead conducted a wide-ranging *chevauchée* from Normandy down to Bordeaux, returning after the death of Henry IV.

Despite the king's recovery in November 1411, his health was still weak and by autumn 1412 he was obviously terminally ill. Prince and king were reconciled and, following the death of Henry IV on 20 March 1413, Prince Henry ascended to the throne as Henry V, and could now carry out his plans for France.

THE HOUR OF DESTINY

Henry V, like his father and their Plantagenet predecessors, sought to resolve the English position in France. In particular, he sought the consolidation of the English possession of the Duchy of Aquitaine in full sovereignty – something that both the Armagnac and Burgundian factions had been willing to offer in their negotiations with the English. Open conflict had broken out again between the two factions in 1413 and so both were anxious to gain the support of the new English king, sending ambassadors to sound him out. Henry V was also diplomatically busy, dispatching a high-level delegation to Charles VI in August 1414 claiming his right to the throne of France, the restitution of the Angevin territories in northern and south-western France and the king's daughter, Katherine of Valois, in marriage along with an enormous dowry of two million crowns. The French, unsurprisingly, rejected this but negotiations continued and a further English embassy was in Paris in February 1415. During the same period Henry had negotiated an agreement with the Duke of Burgundy that he would not interfere in any attempt by Henry to take the crown of France, though Duke

The 1415 campaign

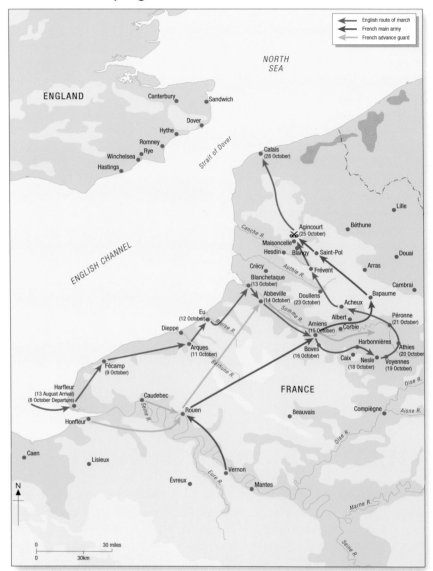

John the Fearless later came to terms with the French king rendering this agreement null and void. This second embassy ended with the same result as the first; although both sides had modified their positions somewhat they were still too far apart – and there remains some doubt that Henry had any intention of it succeeding in any event as it appears that he had decided to undertake an invasion of France by this point.

Preparations and departure

In fact preparations for an invasion had been under way from the very early days of Henry's reign. In May 1413 Henry had forbidden the sale of bows and other weapons to both the Scots and other enemies, while at the same time appointing a fletcher as keeper of the king's arrows in the Tower of London who began to both make and acquire arrows. In September 1414 he also ordered the construction and acquisition of a substantial number of siege engines and guns, while at the same time banning the export of gunpowder from the country.

He also started assembling the major fleet that would be required to ship his army across to France. The king himself possessed a number of ships, including his 'great ships' – among them his flagship the *Trinité Royale* – and was busy building more, but the amount of shipping required dwarfed that available and extra shipping was sought from the Low Countries in early 1415. Henry eventually resorted to seizing all ships – both English and foreign – in English ports in April 1415, and in the end some 1,500 ships were assembled to carry Henry's forces over to France.

These forces now assembled on the French coast ready for the invasion. Henry V's army for the Agincourt campaign was brought together by the indenture system that had replaced the feudal system of raising troops that was common earlier in the medieval period. Essentially, Henry entered into contracts with individual captains who would agree to serve on campaign along with a specified number of men – their retinue – generally categorized as men-at-arms or archers. These captains could range from the great magnates of England, such as the royal dukes, his brothers, who would bring hundreds of men with them in their retinues, to much smaller groups and even individuals themselves. Indeed, the Agincourt force is unusual for the period in terms of the sheer number of indentures issued, with at least 320 individuals recorded. For Thomas, Duke of Clarence's expedition to France in 1412 there had only been three major retinues – that of Clarence himself, the Duke of York and the Earl of Dorset.

The balance of the forces assembled had also changed. Earlier in the Hundred Years War the standard retinue had been fairly equally balanced between men-at-arms and archers, but by the time of the Agincourt campaign this balance had shifted dramatically, so that there were now some three archers for every single man-at-arms. This may have been due to an appreciation of the combat power of English and Welsh archery on the battlefield, something that Henry must have personally appreciated following his experiences at the battle of Shrewsbury, but it might also have to do with the fact that Henry was short of funds, and archers were cheaper to hire than men-at-arms. Although Henry's chancellor, Henry Beaufort, had announced his intentions in the parliament of December 1414 and asked for (and been granted) a double subsidy, only half of this was due in February 1415 with the other half in February 1416. The king therefore made up the shortfall through loans from the city of London and numerous other sources, giving his personal jewels as security.

In all, the army assembled at Southampton consisted of some 12,000 men, out of which perhaps 3,000 would have been men-at-arms. On top of this there would have been numerous non-combatants accompanying the army as servants, miners, carpenters and other support roles. Leading this host were the peers of England. Although their feudal obligations had drifted away over time, it is clear that Henry felt he should be accompanied by the aristocracy of England and, with the exception of some of the marcher lords who were to guard the Scottish border and watch the Welsh, they responded, with some 26 peers providing over 5,000 men for the campaign.

One final embassy from the French came over, meeting Henry just outside Winchester on 1 July 1415. This last set of negotiations went the same way as the others with some substantive discussions over the royal marriage, but the territorial concessions that Henry required were not forthcoming and the French went away empty handed. On 6 July Henry formally declared war on Charles VI, having left his kingdom in the care of his middle brother, John, Duke of Bedford, made his will, and dealt with an attempted aristocratic *coup d'état* (see pp.52–53). His armada set sail for France on Sunday 11 August with Henry's *Trinité Royale* leading the way. Although three ships caught fire and burnt to the water line, swans – one of Henry V's personal devices – were seen swimming after the fleet as they passed the Isle of Wight – a good omen for the operation to come.

The siege of Harfleur

Henry's destination was the Seine Estuary and, more specifically, the town of Harfleur. This fortified port was described by the Burgundian chronicler Enguerran Monstrelet as 'the key to the sea of all Normandy', and as such it made an ideal target for Henry, controlling the traffic down the river Seine giving access to Rouen some 65km (40 miles) up river, and Paris 130km (80 miles) beyond that.

Henry's fleet arrived some 5km (3 miles) away from Harfleur on the afternoon of 13 August and, having summoned a council aboard his flagship, he gave orders that no one was to land before him on pain of death. Henry went ashore early on the 14th and the disembarkation of the English army took a further three days during which time Henry issued

Sailing for France

Henry V (**1**) stands on the after-castle of his ship issuing orders as the French coast appears on the horizon. He has his leg armour and cuirass on, with a heraldic surcoat over it, but is still to don his vambraces and his helm, which is being held by a liveried squire on the far right (**2**). On the left are a herald (**3**) and Sir John Cornwall (**4**) (c.1364–1443), one of the most respected knights of the period. He was part of the first scouting party landed by the English armada and later led the vanguard of the English army from Harfleur to Agincourt before being replaced by the Duke of York. In front of Henry an archer (**5**) bows his head and clasps his hat in front of him. He is dressed for riding, with long boots and spurs, and armed with a falchion and buckler. Henry's ship is the *Trinité Royale*, which at 540 tons was one of the largest ships in northern Europe and the flagship of the fleet. The ship to the right bears a swan, one of Henry's personal symbols, on its sail (**6**).

ordinances for the control of his army, forbidding acts of arson, plundering of church property and granting protection for women, as well as regulating discipline within his army and ordering that all his soldiers should wear the cross of St George as a symbol of identification. Once all this had been done he organized his army into three divisions or 'battles' under Thomas, Duke of Clarence, Edmund, Duke of York, and Henry himself and marched them the short distance to Harfleur, appearing before the town on the 18th.

The town itself was well protected, with a strong wall studded with 26 towers. It was also surrounded with water on three sides, while the defenders had opened sluice gates to flood the valley of the river Lézarde, making it impassable apart from by small boat. There were three gates in the walls – traditionally the weak spots for any form of siege warfare – Montvilliers to the north, Rouen to the south-east and Leure to the south-west. Each of these was protected by a bastion or bulwark projecting beyond the line of the fortifications. The harbour itself was defended by the town wall to the north and a further, higher wall punctuated by defensive turrets and towers facing seaward, while chains and sharpened stakes blocked the entrance on the river itself. The garrison at the start of the siege consisted of around 100 men-at-arms commanded by Jean, Sire d'Estouteville, while 300 reinforcements arrived under Raoul, Sire de Gaucourt, on Sunday 19 August, approaching from beyond the flooded Lézarde Valley so that Henry, who had set up his camp opposite the Leure Gate, could not block their progress. In response to this, and in order to create a proper blockade of the town, Henry sent his brother around the flooded Lézarde Valley, who set up his camp on the hills to the north-east of the town, completing the blockade. The author of the *Gesta Vita Henrici*, an anonymous chaplain who accompanied the expedition, describes what followed next:

Medieval houses lining the banks of the river Lézarde that runs into the Seine. It was Harfleur's strategic position on these waterways that led to it being the target of Henry's armada in 1415. Once the Seine silted up in the 16th century its importance diminished and it was replaced by the newly built port of Le Havre. (Author's collection)

And after orders had been given for a blockade on the sea-ward side by the fleet and on the side of the valley and the fresh-water river by small boats (which would also serve, if necessary, as a means of communication between the king and the duke and their divisions of the army), our king, who sought not war but peace, in order to arm with the shield of innocence the just cause of the great enterprise on which he had embarked, offered in accordance with the twentieth chapter of Deuteronomic law, peace to the besieged if, freely and without coercion, they would open their gates to him and, as was their duty, restore that town, which was a noble and hereditary portion of his crown of England and of his Duchy of Normandy.

The reference to Deuteronomy is significant as the relevant chapter authorized Henry to sack the city in the event of it refusing to surrender, putting all the male inhabitants to the sword and carrying off the women, children and all property as booty. The French commanders summarily rejected this demand and the two sides settled into the traditional pattern of a medieval siege.

A detailed chronology of the siege is difficult to establish from the various sources, but it is clear that Henry was to a large extent relying on the power of his artillery train to overpower the walls and the defenders, enabling him to break into the town hopefully before too much destruction had been done, as it was his intention to garrison and fortify the port to act as another Calais – an armed camp projecting into his Duchy of Normandy. To that end he cleared the suburbs of Harfleur outside the walls and moved his artillery pieces as close as possible through the use of trenches, saps and wooden hoardings to protect his gunners from French crossbow and counter-battery fire. When the artillery was not firing at night, the French defenders sought to repair the damage to their fortifications through the use of any material to hand. At the same time as his artillery was trying to break down the walls, Henry also sought to undermine them by digging tunnels underneath them that would then be collapsed, causing sections of the walls to collapse also. Although Henry made attempts against the Leure Gate, the one opposite his encampment, the moat in front of the wall ensured that this was a difficult task and the area in front of the Duke of Clarence's camp was judged more suitable, as the *Gesta Vita Henrici* describes:

And while these activities were in progress, the king decided to attack by means of mines and, after a 'sow' had been made ready, to undermine with passages below ground the walls on the Duke

Little remains of the medieval fortifications of Harfleur, and the town is now an industrial suburb of the much larger port of Le Havre. However, medieval houses from the time of the siege do still remain, as does the parish church of Saint-Martin, which dates from the 15th century. (Author's collection)

of Clarence's side. But this operation (which, contrary to the teaching of Master Giles, was begun in full view of the enemy since it could not be accomplished in any other way at any other point on account of the nearness of the hill and for other reasons), having twice been foiled by hard work of the enemy, who used counter-mines and other technical skills in opposition to ours, and recommenced yet a third time, brought no advantage at all.

The French were resisting much harder than Henry had anticipated. In a letter dated 3 September to the citizens of Bordeaux, one of the senior clerks of his household stated that the town would be in his hands within eight days and that the king would then proceed to Dieppe, Rouen and Paris. Both these claims would prove to be false as the siege dragged on into its third week, with the French countering all English attempts to break through their fortifications. September also saw a new threat develop in the English camp as disease spread throughout the army – it was the 'bloody flux': dysentery.

The presence of such a large number of troops in such a confined area, with all the effluent and other waste products that entailed, combined with the damp, low-lying nature of the ground and the hot, humid weather, proved to be a perfect breeding ground for the disease and it spread rapidly throughout the army, affecting even the highest of nobles and courtiers. On 10 September Richard Courtenay, Bishop of Norwich, contracted the disease and by the 15th he was dead, with Henry V himself attending him on his deathbed. On the 18th Michael de la Pole, Earl of Suffolk, died with his title going to his eldest son, also named Michael, who was serving in his father's retinue. By this stage the siege had also moved on to a new stage as, on the 15th, a French sally from the Leure Gate caught the defenders off guard, as the *Gesta Vita Henrici* relates:

> And on the same day there occurred another event which was sufficiently serious to cause the king disquiet; for our adversaries who were on guard at the strongest barbican made a sally against our guard facing them and, because

The siege of Harfleur

Set in the siege lines attacking the Leure Gate that lies in the background, the bastion in front of the gate is out of sight, hidden by the English palisade. At the centre is the entrance to an English earthwork, with a sapper struggling out with a barrow of earth and another making his way into the siege works. At left Sir John Holland discusses the progress of the siege with one of his engineer captains. Along with Sir John Cornwall and Sir William Porter, Sir John Holland was responsible for this sector of the English siege works and was surprised by a sudden attack on the fortifications on 15 September. This attack was revenged the following day when Sir John Holland launched an attack on the barbican in front of the Leure Garte, setting fire to it and forcing the French to retreat – an act that precipitated the final surrender of the town. To the right, two of the labourers appear to be suffering from the dysentery that was to cut a huge swathe through Henry's fighting forces.

of the inattention and indolence of our men, set fire to their defences. But eventually, by God's will, the fire was extinguished and the enemy put to flight without our men being seriously hurt. The enemy, however, taunted us with being only half-awake and lazy, in that when on watch we had not been able to keep a better look-out.

This assault provoked an immediate response and, the following day, Sir John Holland, who was one of the commanders of the men facing the Leure Gate and whose command had been attacked the previous day, sought to make amends by launching an attack on the bastion or bulwark that protected the Leure Gate. This attack, unlike the many that preceded it, proved successful and the French defenders were burnt out of their position and driven back behind the main walls. Following up on this success, Henry entered negotiations with the French defenders once more, offering them terms for surrender. Raoul de Gaucourt refused once again and Henry planned an all-out assault on the town for the following day; by this stage the townspeople had had enough and sent a message to Thomas, Duke of Clarence, that they were wiling to come to terms. Realizing that their position was now untenable, de Gaucourt and d'Estouteville now accepted that should neither the King or the Dauphin come into sight by 22 September with a relieving army then they would surrender Harfleur to Henry. A messenger was sent from Harfleur to Vernon, where a French army was being assembled, but was told that it was too soon for them to intervene, and so Harfleur was lost. The *Gesta Vita Henrici* describes the events of the surrender on Sunday 22 September:

> And when, neither at the appointed hour on the following Sunday nor before, the French king, the Dauphin, or anyone else had offered to raise the siege, our king straightaway ascended his royal throne, over which was spread cloth of gold and fine linen, in a pavilion at the top of the hill in front of the town, and he was attended by men of high rank, his magnates and nobles, in large number and wearing their richest apparel; and to his right, carried on a staff by Sir Gilbert Umfraville, was his triumphal helm bearing his crown. From the town there came into his presence the aforesaid [Raoul], Sire de Gaucourt, accompanied by those persons who had previously sworn to keep the agreements, and he restored to the king the keys of the town and at the same time surrendered himself and the townspeople to his mercy.

Henry himself didn't enter the town until Monday 23 September, when he came barefoot and walked to the parish church to pray for his victory. The surviving men-at-arms and knights from the garrison were paroled to surrender to the king at Calais on 11 November to be ransomed, and the townspeople were allowed to keep their possessions (though not their property) if they swore obedience to Henry; those who did not were held for ransom while all of the poorest were expelled. The town of Harfleur was to be remade with English colonists.

Henry had his conquest, but it had come at a price. As many as 2,000 of his men had perished of dysentery with as many as 2,000 more having to be sent home, including his brother, Thomas, Duke of Clarence, and one of his senior commanders, Thomas, Earl of Arundel, who died on 13 October back in England. Henry had also decided to garrison Harfleur strongly, leaving some 1,200 men, 900 archers and 300 men-at-arms under the command of Thomas Beaufort, Earl of Dorset. This all ensured that his force was greatly reduced from the 12,000 or so that had crossed the channel with him. A number of different chroniclers list the figures of 900 men-at-arms and 5,000 archers accompanying the king on the campaign after the siege of Harfleur, though this may be on the low side, and Anne Curry has estimated that the force with Henry was a few hundred men either side of 9,000. On 27 September Henry challenged (through Raoul de Gaucourt) the Dauphin, Louis, to a personal duel to settle the issues between the English and French monarchies, and while waiting for a response that was never to come Henry planed his next move. The letter to Bordeaux of 3 September had stated that Henry would advance through Normandy before going on to Paris. This was now impossible due to his straightened circumstances, but he had the option of heading south-west towards Bordeaux and home, much as Clarence had done in 1412, or heading through his Duchy of Normandy towards Calais. Against the wishes of his council he chose this latter option.

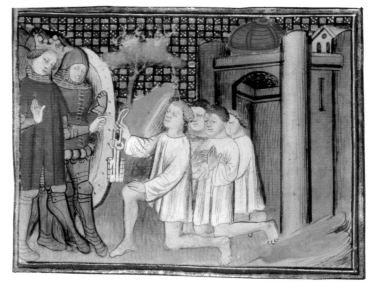

Edward III accepts the surrender of the burghers of Calais in 1347, led by Eustache de Saint-Pierre. This is a manuscript illustration from the *Chroniques* of Jean Froissart, and shows the aftermath of a medieval siege such as that at Harfleur. Following its capture by Edward III, Calais proved to be the most long-lasting English base in France, only finally falling to the French in 1558. (akg-images/ Erich Lessing)

The march to Agincourt

Between 6 and 8 October (the date varies between the sources) Henry and the remnants of his army left Harfleur for their march to Calais. The journey was supposed to take eight days, which sounds optimistic considering the distance was 232km (144 miles). The journey was contested along the way almost immediately, with a party of crossbowmen coming out of Montvilliers (5km [3 miles] north of Harfleur) to skirmish with the army, a pattern that was to be repeated along the march. The English army was organized into three battles, as was customary, with the vanguard under the command of Sir Gilbert Umfraville and Sir John Cornwall, while the King himself, along with Humphrey, Duke of Gloucester, and Sir John Holland led the main body, while the Duke of York and Earl of Oxford led the rearguard. The army passed Fécamp on the 9th, and French chroniclers accuse the English of sacking the abbey there. On the 11th they reached the town and castle of Arques, just inland from Dieppe, and Henry managed to acquire some supplies for his army through intimidating the garrison of the castle with the threat of sacking their town and fortifications. This policy again proved effective at his next stop, the town of Eu on 12 October when, following a skirmish, the French again submitted and provided supplies of bread and wine. Henry's intention was to cross the river Somme at Blanchetaque, where Edward III had forced a crossing during the Crécy campaign in 1346. He had even ordered a force of 300 men southwards out of Calais to secure his passage. However, here he found his crossing opposed on 13 October and had to make new arrangements, as Tito Livio, author of the *Vita Henrici Quinti* of *c*.1438 describes: 'Then the English reached the passage of the River Somme which the French called Blanchetaque. Because it had been defended in advance by the enemy by means of sharp stakes fixed close together, it allowed the English no chance of crossing. Thus they had to move upstream in search of another crossing.'

Although the French had been slow to react to the English siege of Harfleur they had now decided to make their move. Charles d'Albret, the Constable of France, and Marshal Boucicaut had commanded observation forces during the siege of Harfleur at Honfleur and Caudebec respectively. Following the fall of Harfleur they had returned to Rouen where a French army was being assembled, with both the King and Dauphin arriving there by 12 October. They had then formed part of an advance guard, as large as 6,000 strong, that had crossed the Somme, based itself at Abbeville and now denied the crossing to Henry and his army.

Henry was now forced to turn inland in an attempt to find an unguarded crossing point so he could resume his march on Calais, though he now knew that his supplies would not last the distance. The English force followed the river Somme south-eastwards, skirting around the fortified city of Abbeville, which held substantial French forces, who were also shadowing the English progress along the other bank of the Somme. On the 15th they passed the city of Amiens, while on the 16th they reached Boves, where Henry was able to gain supplies for his army by threatening to sack the place, much as he had done at Arques and Eu earlier in the march. The following day the army pushed on towards Corbie, where there was a large-scale sortie by the French against the English column. This was pushed back and French prisoners taken, from whom Henry learnt something of the French battle plans and sought to counter them to some extent, as the *Gesta Henrici Quinti* relates:

> Meanwhile as a result of information divulged by some prisoners, a rumour went the rounds of the army that the enemy command had assigned certain squadrons of cavalry, many hundreds strong and mounted on barded horses, to break the formation and resistance of our archers when they engaged us in battle. The king, therefore, had it proclaimed throughout the army that every archer was to prepare and fashion for himself a stake or staff, square or round, but six feet long, of sufficient thickness, and sharpened at both ends; and he commanded that whenever the French army drew near to do battle and to break

The village of Béthencourt-sur-Somme lies on the banks of the river Somme and it was here, and at Voyennes, that Henry V and his army forced a crossing of the river early on the morning of 19 October, thus enabling him to steal a march on the French advance guard, who were forced to follow the loop of the Somme via Péronne. (Hektor)

their ranks by such columns of horse, all the archers were to drive in their stakes… so that the cavalry, when their charge had brought them close and in sight of the stakes would either withdraw in great fear or, reckless of their own safety, run the risk of having both horses and riders impaled.

By this point the main French army was probably on the move from Rouen, reaching Amiens once the English forces had passed further to the south. Henry had to make a bold decision in order to get his men across the Somme, and decided to cut off a great loop of the river, heading directly towards the village of Ham. This would enable him to get ahead of the French shadowing force, which would be forced to follow the long loop of the Somme along the north bank. On the 18th they reached the village of Nesle, and, on the 19th, crossing points were discovered between the hamlets of Voyennes and Béthencourt-sur-Somme.

The French had damaged the approaches to these crossings, but they were intact enough to allow the English to cross cautiously, which the vanguard did on the morning of the 19th under the command of Sir Gilbert Umfraville and Sir John Cornwall. Although the French attempted to interfere with the crossing, by the time they had reacted too large a force of English troops had already crossed and the main army was over the river by late afternoon, marching on to Athies where they made camp.

Although across the river, they were by no means out of danger and on the 20th heralds came from the French camp offering battle. Henry replied that he intended to march his army to Calais, and that the Princes of France could find him in the open fields. From this point on the army marched as if they might

encounter battle at any moment, with their armour on and coats of arms displayed. Setting off on the 21st, the English passed Péronne to the left and, shortly afterwards, crossed over the tracks left by a large host – this was certainly the main French army which, having arrived at Amiens, was now moving on towards Bapaume. From this point on the French could cut the English army off at any point they wanted, blocking the main road to Calais with ease. The English pressed on, spending the night in the Mametz–Fricourt area on the battlefield of the Somme of 1916. On the 22nd they reached Acheux, and Doullens on the 23rd. By the evening of the 24th the English had reached the village of Maisoncelle, where they found the combined French force ahead of them camped between the villages of Agincourt and Rousseauville, blocking the road to Calais and forcing the English to battle the following day.

Maisoncelle was the location of the English camp the night before the battle, and it was from here that they advanced to take up their first position on the morning of 25 October 1415. The view here is from the village itself. (Author's collection)

The battle of Agincourt

There may well have been a degree of negotiation between the English and French the night and morning before the battle, and some French sources claim that Henry was willing to accept a considerably reduced portion of his original territorial demands. However, no agreement was met and the armies were placed in their battle formations.

The chaplain author of the *Gesta Henrici Quinti* describes how Henry arrayed his army in the morning:

> And meanwhile our king, offering praises to God and hearing masses, made ready for the field, which was at no great distance from his quarters, and, in want of numbers, he drew up only a single line of battle, placing his vanguard, commanded by the Duke of York, as a wing on the right and the rearguard, commanded by Lord Camoys, as a wing on the left; and he positioned 'wedges' of his archers in between each 'battle' and had them drive their stakes in front of them, as previously arranged in case of a cavalry charge.

This was in effect a change in command, with Sir Gilbert Umfraville and Sir John Cornwall being removed from command owing, as the chroniclers state, to the Duke of York's fervent desire to lead the vanguard. His place as commander of the rearguard was taken by the experienced Lord Camoys. The three battles were drawn up in a single line, with the baggage and non-combatants behind. This meant there was no reserve at all; Henry had committed all of his men to the line of battle. The role of the English archers in the battle has caused some controversy over the years. The chronicle written by the chaplain quoted above states that they were deployed as wedges between the three divisions of men-at-arms. However, some historians, notably Jim Bradbury (*The Medieval Archer* Boydell & Brewer: Woodbridge, 1985), have claimed that this would have been a most unusual deployment for the era, and would have weakened the line of men-at-arms considerably. Instead they suggest that the archers were deployed on the flanks, behind their line of stakes, enabling them to provide a flanking fire on the French forces while at the same time leaving the line of men-at-arms unbroken.

The battlefield at Agincourt is well commemorated by a museum in the village itself and memorials and a Calvary on the field. These models of archers line the road from Agincourt to Tramecourt, which runs just in front of where the French front line would have been. (Author's collection)

For the French there survives a battle plan devised to deal with the English threat; although it was only applicable to the smaller advanced force under the command of Marshal Boucicaut and Constable d'Albret it does highlight many of the tactics used by the French in the actual battle itself. They intended to use two divisions of mounted troops to the flanks and rear of the army to encircle and neutralize the English archers, and to attack the baggage train and rear of the English army, while the main body of men-at-arms was to advance in the centre, protected to the flanks by crossbowmen and other missile troops that were available.

The actual formation adopted by the French on the day of the battle is strikingly similar, with the three central battles of men-at-arms lined up one in front of each other. The first two consisted of dismounted men-at-arms while the third was mounted. Two further units of mounted troops were mounted on the flanks, while French crossbowmen and other missile troops appear to have played little part in the battle. While the basic formation of the French forces appears to be clear, the numbers involved are to a large extent uncertain. The French certainly outnumbered the English, but to what extent is debatable. A recent study by Anne Curry (*Agincourt: A New History* Tempus: Stroud, 2006) argues that the numbers involved are much closer than previous historians have claimed, and that the French forces may have only totalled 12,000 compared to an English figure of 9,000. The various English and French chronicles give any figure from 8,000 to 150,000, with the total of 60,000 occurring frequently. The Burgundian chronicler Enguerran Monstrelet breaks down the French army in some detail, with 13,500 men in the first battle, a similar number in the main battle and the rest in the third, excepting two forces of 800 and 1,600 cavalry on the flanks, giving a grand total for the French of between 35,000 and 40,000. While the numbers may be uncertain, what is clear is that the English forces had a preponderance of archers

The battle of Agincourt, 25 October 1415

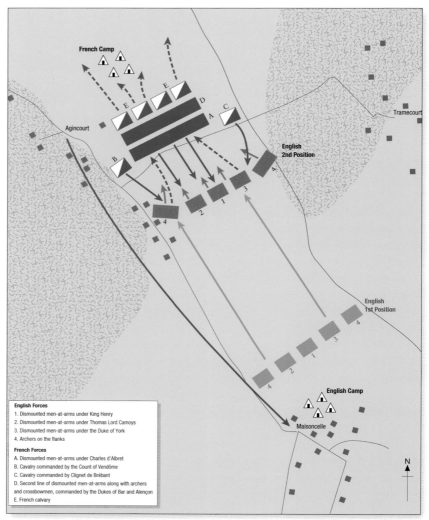

English Forces
1. Dismounted men-at-arms under King Henry
2. Dismounted men-at-arms under Thomas Lord Camoys
3. Dismounted men-at-arms under the Duke of York
4. Archers on the flanks

French Forces
A. Dismounted men-at-arms under Charles d'Albret
B. Cavalry commanded by the Count of Vendôme
C. Cavalry commanded by Clignet de Brébant
D. Second line of dismounted men-at-arms along with archers and crossbowmen, commanded by the Dukes of Bar and Alençon
E. French calvary

as opposed to men-at-arms, while the French forces were much more traditionally based upon the heavily armoured men-at-arms as the centre point of their fighting force.

The French system of command and control was by no means as clear cut as that of the English, with the advance guard commanded by Constable d'Albret and Marshal Boucicaut along with the Dukes of Orléans and Bourbon, as well as the Counts of Eu and Richemont. The main body was under the Dukes of Bar and Alençon and the Counts of Nevers, Vaudemont, Blaumont, Salines Grand-pré and Roussy, the rearguard under the Counts of Dammartin and Fauquembergue, while the forces on the flanks were led by the Count of Vendôme and Clignet de Brébant. This complexity of the command structure led to French commentators blaming it for the defeat that followed, as described by the anonymous monk of Saint-Denis:

In the absence of the king of France and the dukes of Guienne, Brittany and Burgundy, the other princes had taken charge of the conduct of the war. There is no doubt that they would have brought it to a happy conclusion if they had not shown so much disdain for the small number of the enemy and if they had not engaged in the battle so impetuously, despite the advice of knights who were worth listening to because of their age and experience... When it came to putting the army into battle formation (as is always the usage before coming to blows) each of the leaders claimed for himself the honour of leading the vanguard. This led to considerable debate and so that there could be some agreement, they came to the rather unfortunate conclusion that they should all place themselves in the front line.

With the armies arranged, both sides stayed in their positions – the French between the villages of Agincourt and Tramecourt while the English line of battle was situated just outside of their camp at Maisoncelle. When it came to a stand off, however, the English had much more to lose and Henry decided to advance his men towards the French line, moving from around 1,000m (3,280ft) away to within around 300m (1,000ft), as the *St Albans Chronicle* written by Thomas Walsingham relates:

> Because of the muddiness of the place, however, the French did not wish to proceed too far into the field. They waited about to see what our men, whom they held cheap, intended to do. Between each of the two armies the field lay, scarcely 1,000 paces in extent... Because the French were holding their position without moving it was necessary for the English, if they wished to come to grips with the enemy, to traverse the middle ground on foot, burdened with their arms.

Somewhat surprisingly, this advance appears to have been largely uncontested by the French, and the English were able to take up their second position unmolested, which put them within range of bowshot of the French line and also gave them thick woods to both protect the archers on the flanks and narrow the frontage available for any French advance.

Once they had taken up this new position, Sir Thomas Erpingham, steward of the Royal household and one of the most experienced officers in Henry's army, gave the archers the order to fire and the 5,000 men, positioned on both flanks, complied. This appears to have provoked the French cavalry into launching a charge at the archers' positions. However, a combination of the heavy going over ploughed fields, the incessant arrow fire and the fact they couldn't get round the flanks of the archers because of the woods meant that the French cavalry were driven back. The charge was also not

This view of the Agincourt battlefield is taken from the Agincourt–Tramecourt road looking towards the English camp at Maisoncelle. It is over this ground that the English army advanced to take up their second position and launch the missile attack that would start the battle. (Author's collection)

helped by the fact that only a small proportion of the 2,400 cavalry on the flanks actually participated in it, less than 500, so there was no weight behind the move. The chronicler Jean Juvenal des Ursins describes what happened to the charge:

> The French were heavily armed and sank into the ground right to the thick of their legs, which caused them much travail for they could scarcely move their legs and pull them out of the ground. They began to march until arrowfire occurred from both sides. Then the lords on horseback, bravely and most valiantly wanted to attack the archers who began to aim against the cavalry and their horses with great fervour. When the horses felt themselves pierced by arrows, they could no longer be controlled by their riders in the advance. The horses turned and it seems that those who were mounted on them fled, or so is the opinion and belief of some, and they were very much blamed for this.

Not only did the French cavalry flee, they also ploughed headlong into the advancing French first and second battles, which had started their advance. They were marching towards the English position and struggling through the mud, now churned up even further by the French cavalry charge, when the impact of the retreating horse disrupted their cohesion even more. The English archers were still firing at them from their flanking positions, forcing the men-at-arms to stay 'buttoned up' in their full armour protection, causing further stress and disorientation. They eventually reached the English line and pushed it back through sheer weight of numbers, but this same numerical superiority was also causing the French lines to pile up on each other and restricted their freedom of movement, while the archers still tormented them from the flanks and, when they ran out of arrows, intervened more directly on the battlefield, as the Burgundian chronicler Enguerran Monstrelet relates:

> Because of the strength of the arrow fire and their fear of it, most of the others doubled back into the French vanguard, causing great disarray and breaking the line in many places, making them fall back onto the ground which had been newly sown. The horses had been so troubled by the arrow shot of the English archers that they could not hold or control them. As a result the vanguard fell into disorder and countless numbers of men-at-arms began to fall. Those on horseback were so afraid of death that they put themselves into flight away from the enemy. Because of the example they set many of the French left the field in flight.
>
> Soon afterwards the English fell upon them body on body. Dropping their bows and arrows to the ground, they took up their swords, axes, hammers, falchions and other weapons of war. With great blows they killed the French who fell dead to the ground. In doing this they came so far forward that they almost reached the main battle, which was following in behind the vanguard. After the English archers the King of England followed up by marching in with all his men-at-arms in great strength.

The intervention of the lightly armoured and manoeuvrable English archers appears to have been crucial in what was a hard-fought battle. Sources on both sides relate that piles of bodies built up around the various royal and aristocratic standards in the English front line, with Henry himself supposed to have protected the wounded body of his brother Humphrey, Duke of Gloucester, and to have lost a fleuret from the gold crown of his helmet.

Despite the fierce nature of the fighting, the first two French battles were defeated and their leaders either killed or captured. However, the final and most controversial act of the battle was yet to come. When the English began rounding up their numerous prisoners the rumour went round that the as-yet-uncommitted French third battle was entering the fray. This third force was so numerous as to be a threat to the English position, particularly as they had a large number of prisoners to their rear. At the same time a further French cavalry force attacked the English baggage and camp, capturing part of the royal treasure.

A highly stylized 15th-century illustration of the battle of Agincourt, showing the castle in the background, from the *Abrege de la Chronique d'Enguerrand de Monstrelet* (Ms.français 2680, fol.208r) held in the Bibliothèque Nationale, Paris. Enguerran Monstrelet was a Burgundian chronicler active at the court of Philip the Good, Duke of Burgundy. (akg-images/Jerome da Cunha)

A view of the Agincourt battlefield looking from Maisoncelle towards the village of Tramecourt. At the time of the battle the woods on both sides of the battle were much thicker and provided a flank defence for Henry's army. (Author's collection)

These events led to Henry ordering the killing of the French prisoners, apart from those of particularly noble birth. According to the chronicler Jean de Waurin: 'When the king was told no-one was willing to kill his prisoners he appointed a gentleman with 200 archers to the task, commanding him that all the prisoners be killed. The esquire carried out the order of the king which was a most pitiable matter. For in cold blood, all those noble Frenchman were killed and had their heads and faces cut, which was an amazing sight to see.' It is uncertain how many prisoners were killed, but the French chroniclers suggest over 1,000. The French third battle never intervened in the battle, slipping away and leaving the field to the English. Enguerran Monstrelet again describes the reaction:

> Whilst his men were busy in stripping and robbing those who had been killed, he
> summoned the herald of the king of France, the king at arms called Mountjoye,

The battle of Agincourt

This scene depicts the critical point of the battle. The French men-at-arms have crossed the field and are embroiled with the English line, while the English archers are beginning to engage from the flank in an assault that contributed a great deal to the eventual English victory. In the centre is Henry himself, with his crown on top of his unvisored great basinet. To his left is Sir Thomas Erpingham, who gave the order for the archers to fire their first volley, and some way to his right is Humphrey, Duke of Gloucester. Behind Henry fly the banners associated with Agincourt (from left to right): Henry's personal standard, the cross of St George, the Holy Trinity, and the standards of Edward the Confessor and St Edmund. Advancing towards Henry is Jean, Sire de Croy, who, along with his retinue, made a pact to kill Henry and supposedly hacked off part of his crown. On the ground in the centre is a French knight struggling with an English archer, who is trying to stab him through his open visor, while to the right another French knight has felt the full force of one of the heavy mallets wielded by the lightly armoured archers.

along with several other heralds both French and English, and said to them, 'It is not we who have caused this killing but God the Almighty, on account of the sins of the French, for so we believe.' Later when he asked them to whom the victory should be accorded, to him or to the king of France. Mountjoye replied that to him was the victory and not the king of France. Then the king asked him the name of the castle which he could see close by. They answered it was called Agincourt. 'As all battles', the king said, ought to take their name from the nearest fortress, village or town where they happened, this battle from henceforth and for ever more will be called the battle of Agincourt.'

The view from the Agincourt–Tramecourt road looking back towards the French lines. The French advanced across this ground, which had been recently ploughed, under constant arrow fire from the English archers. (Author's collection)

The casualties on the French side were horrific. The *Gesta Henrici Quinti* lists French aristocratic fatalities as three dukes – those of Alençon, Bar and Brabant – five counts, more than 90 barons and bannerets and upwards of 1,500 knights. On top of these casualties there were also a number of high-ranking prisoners, including Marshal Boucicaut, the Dukes of Orléans and Bourbon, and the Counts of Eu, Richemont and Vendôme. On the English side the only notable casualties were Edward, Duke of York, and Michael de la Pole, Earl of Suffolk, whose father had died of dysentery at Harfleur.

It is no wonder, given the scale of the English victory, that some commentators ascribed it to mystical causes. One such was Thomas Elmham, author of the *Liber Metricus de Henrico Quinto*: 'In the field St George was seen fighting in the battle on the side of the English. The Virgin, the handmaiden

A late 15th-century illustration of the battle of Agincourt from *Les Vigiles de Charles VII* by Martial d'Auvergne (Ms. francais 5054, fol.11) held in the Bibliothèque Nationale, Paris. This illustration focuses on the mêlée following the French assault and depicts an English man-at-arms leading bound French prisoners away, their fate as-yet unknown. (akg-images)

A monument to the dead of the battle of Agincourt (or Azincourt) stands just outside the village of Maisoncelle, along with a map detailing the events of the battle. (Author's collection)

of the almighty, protected the English. All the glory be given to her not us. St Maurice took Harfleur, St Crispin carried the battle of Agincourt.' This has an interesting parallel in later history when the author Arthur Machen published an account of the battle of Mons on 29 September 1914 that has the archers of Agincourt assisting the British Expeditionary Force in the field. Though intended as a fiction, many took this as a true account of events.

With the battle won and the French dispersed, Henry withdrew with his forces to Maisoncelle for the night before undertaking a three-day trek to Calais, where he waited for a fortnight before returning to Dover on 16 November and then London where his great victory was duly celebrated in some style.

This was in fact just one step in the process of conquest that would carve out a Lancastrian kingdom in France, and the hardest part was yet to come.

Above: These two views of the battlefield are taken from Rousseauville, which lay to the rear of the French camp. The first looks towards Agincourt on the right, while the second looks towards Tramecourt to the left. The woods narrowed the space available for the French advance and provided protection for the English flanks. (Author's collection)

The conquest of Normandy

Shakespeare moves swiftly from the aftermath of the battle of Agincourt to the signing of the Treaty of Troyes; in reality five years separated these two events, and much of that time would be spent in hard campaigning. From the start of his second expedition to France in July 1417 to the time of his death in 1422, Henry spent only five months in England – the rest of the time he was in France, and mostly on campaign.

One of the principal targets of Henry's campaign in 1417 was Caen, Normandy's second town. This structure, the Exchequer Hall in the Ducal Castle, built by Henry I in the 12th century, is the only surviving structure of the medieval castle. (Author's collection)

English campaigns in France, 1417–20

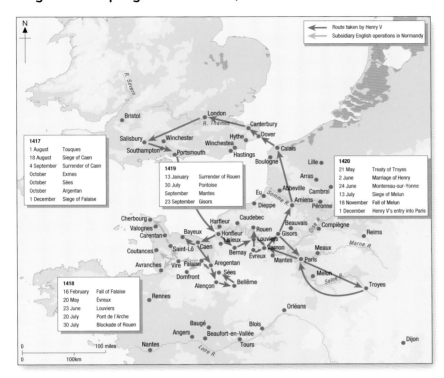

Route taken by Henry V
Subsidiary English operations in Normandy

1417
1 August	Touques
18 August	Siege of Caen
4 September	Surrender of Caen
October	Exmes
October	Sées
October	Argentan
1 December	Siege of Falaise

1418
16 February	Fall of Falaise
20 May	Évreux
23 June	Louviers
20 July	Pont de l'Arche
30 July	Blockade of Rouen

1419
13 January	Surrender of Rouen
30 July	Pontoise
September	Mantes
23 September	Gisors

1420
21 May	Treaty of Troyes
2 June	Marriage of Henry
24 June	Montereau-sur-Yonne
13 July	Siege of Melun
18 November	Fall of Melun
1 December	Henry V's entry into Paris

The Tour Leroy formed part of the medieval fortifications of Caen, standing on the banks of the river Odon, now covered over. It was connected by a chain to a tower on the other bank of the Odon and formed part of the wall of the old town. (Author's collection)

During 1416 Henry entertained the Holy Roman Emperor, Sigismund, who, in a sign of how far Henry's status had risen following his victory at Agincourt, signed the Treaty of Canterbury with the English king on 15 August 1416, which acknowledged Henry's 'just rights' in France. Following this the King and Emperor met with the Duke of Burgundy in Calais, at which point an extension of the Anglo-Burgundian truce for six months was agreed, and further concessions were hinted at. An agreement was also reached with the Duke of Brittany in April 1417 that would keep the Bretons out of the forthcoming campaign. Henry could now prepare for his forthcoming campaign, with parliament and church both providing generous subsidies for the military expedition, while Henry borrowed against his crown jewels once more. In February, Henry ordered feathers plucked from geese throughout England and sent to the Tower of London, and by July his preparations were complete.

Arguably the most important victory of the whole campaign was fought and won in Henry's absence. His brother, John, Duke of Bedford, defeated a French fleet in the Seine Estuary on 22 July 1416; this safeguarded the English conquest of Harfleur and broke the French blockade of the port, thus enabling Henry to have a solid base of supply when he launched his campaign the following year.

The remnants of the keep of the Ducal Castle, Caen. The centrepiece of the fortifications of Caen – the keep – was built by William the Conqueror from 1060 onwards. (Author's collection)

Henry's force was remarkably similar in size to that taken across for the Agincourt campaign – as many as 12,000 strong with the balance of forces heavily in favour of archers. The men were all contracted to serve for a year, and the invasion fleet set sail on 30 July, landing in France on 1 August at Touques, capturing the castle there within four days, the first step in a programme of conquest that would enable Henry to recover 'his' Duchy of Normandy. The principal target of the early days of his campaign was the town of Caen, which along with Rouen was the most important town in Normandy and a vital administrative centre. Henry put the town under siege on 18 August and, with the walls having been breached by his artillery, a full assault was ordered on 4 September. Henry again split his forces, with a portion under the Duke of Clarence on the far side of the town, with Henry and his men on the near side. The fighting was fierce as the defenders sought to deny the English their walls, as described in the *The First English Life of Henry V*:

One of the entrances to the Ducal Castle at Caen. Although the town of Caen fell to the English on 4 September amidst great slaughter, the castle held out for a further 16 days and could have held out for much longer. However, Henry offered generous terms and the demoralized garrison surrendered. (Author's collection)

The Englishmen raysed there ladders to the walls, and assayled to skale them wth all the diligence they coulde; but many of them were foorwth cast backwards into the ditch, and there laders wth them. Then on all parts the Englishmen assended the walls and foorthwth fought right manly, and laboured right sore to gett the Towne; and they of the Towne eneuored them as busily, and not wth lesse laboure, by shott and castinge of stones, by sheddinge of skaldinge water and boylinge pich and oyle upon the Englishmen to resist theire enterprise; but allwaies, as one ladder was ouerthrowne and cast from the walls, many other more ardently were sett upp in his place.

However, the Duke of Clarence had more luck and managed to force his way into the town:

The imposing walls of the Ducal Castle, Caen. Apart from the immense château, Caen boasted walls studded with 32 towers and 12 fortified gates. (Author's collection)

In an other place farr from the Kinge was the noble Duke of Clarence, wch also wth great vigor assaulted the Towne on his part: whose strength the Frenchmen, neither by the helpe of there highe walls, there deepe ditches, by castinge of stones, by shott, by helpe of there whot water, boylinge pitch or oyle, nor by no manner of strength or pollicie might resist them, but that they were so sore oppressed by the Duke and of his people, wch in maruelous multitude and incredible audacitie and manhoode scaled the walls: and they were constrained to forsake the walls and to flye into the Towne.

What followed was a brutal sack of the town, with only the churches being spared. The sack of Caen may well have been a calculated act of brutality to cow the other Norman towns into submission, and it certainly had this effect as Henry rapidly struck to the south, taking the towns of Exmes, Sées, Argentan

Following the fall of Caen, Henry pressed southwards to the southern borders of Normandy, capturing towns en route including Sées. Shown here is the chapter house of the cathedral that dominates the town. (Author's collection)

The towers of the Église Saint-Etienne, the abbey church of the Abbaye-aux-Hommes constructed by William the Conqueror in Caen. In 1417 the abbey lay outside the city walls and was to provide a handy gun platform for Henry's assaulting forces. (Author's collection)

and Alençon in a 15-day campaign, which in turn led to a further meeting and truce with the Duke of Brittany.

Henry turned north again and, carrying on his campaigning throughout the winter, besieged the town and fortress of Falaise, while at the same time dispatching his brother Humphrey, Duke of Gloucester, to subdue the Cotentin Peninsula and capture the port of Cherbourg.

By the spring of 1418 Henry had largely completed the conquest of lower Normandy and was free to turn to Rouen, the most important target of his campaigns and the ancient capital of Normandy.

Having captured the vital crossing point of the Somme at Pont de l'Arche on 20 July 1418, Rouen was effectively surrounded by the English forces on 30 July, with fortified camps established opposite the entrances to the city, linked to each other with trenches, while the whole of Rouen was surrounded by a deep ditch studded with stakes. This time Henry's artillery was not sufficient to batter the walls to pieces so an assault could be made; Rouen would have to be starved into submission.

By October food was starting to run short in the city, leading to desperate measures. The author of the *The First English Life of Henry V* describes the scene:

> Thus this prudent Prince, more streightlie oppressinge the Cittie them tofore, made sufficient defences on all parts to saue his hoast from all perrills of sodaine inuasions; by means whereof the Cittie inualished hunger, in so much that in default of other meattes they were constrained first to devide amongst them there horses, and also there dogs, and then there catts, ratts and myse, and generally all thinges that might be gotten; and of that vile sustenance the people coulde not haue enoughe but that when all these and al other things that were comestible were consumed and eaten, then the plague of famine entered the Cittie.

As the famine took hold the defenders took the decision to expel all those not directly involved in the defence – the sick and infirm, elderly, women and children. However, Henry was unwilling to let these non-combatants through his siege lines and, apart from a charitable gesture on Christmas Day, they were left to starve to death, trapped between the walls of Rouen and the English lines. The position in the city was now becoming desperate and there was still no French relief force in sight. On 13 January the city agreed to surrender on the 19th if no relief force was in sight and, on the 19th, the keys were duly handed over, and Henry entered the town on the 20th with all due pomp and ceremony. Much as with the fall of Caen, the loss of Rouen caused the collapse of the French position in upper Normandy, before an event took place in September that would transform the nature of the campaign.

Throughout the Agincourt campaign the Burgundian and Armagnac factions had been unable to settle their differences in the face of the external threat posed by the English, and the renewed English campaign of 1417–19 proved to be no different. In fact John the Fearless, Duke of Burgundy, took advantage of the chaos caused by the English invasion to launch an attack on Armagnac possessions in the Seine region in spring 1418 and, on 29 May, Burgundian forces captured Paris, massacring Armagnac supporters and gaining control of the royal family with the exception of the Dauphin who managed to escape. This now placed the Duke of Burgundy at the head of the French Government and in opposition to the English invasion, and Burgundian troops were present at the defence of Pont de l'Arche in July 1418. Following the

Henry's ultimate destination in his push southwards from Caen was the town of Alençon, which put up no resistance to his forces despite being well prepared for a siege. (Author's collection)

fall of Rouen negotiations took place between the Duke, Queen Isabeau, Princess Katherine and Henry V between Mantes and Pontoise (Charles VI was too unwell to attend). These negotiations broke down and the Burgundians signed the Treaty of Pouilly with the Armagnacs, ending their war and uniting them against the English. In response Henry took the town of Pontoise, just 27km (17 miles) from Paris, which forced the French royal family and the Duke of Burgundy to move to the town of Troyes.

A meeting between the Duke of Burgundy and the Dauphin at Montereau on 10 September 1419 ended with the assassination of the Duke by the Dauphin's men, driving the Burgundian faction headlong into the arms of Henry V, who realized that his moment of opportunity had come.

Following a series of complex negotiations, Henry agreed to a full and final settlement of the war between France and England; he would marry Princess

Katherine and be appointed heir to the throne of France, which Charles VI would keep for the remainder of his life. Henry would also be regent of France for his father-in-law while he was indisposed. The Dauphin would be completely disinherited. This was all agreed on Christmas Day 1419 and ratified in the Treaty of Troyes, signed on 21 May 1420, following which Henry was married to Katherine and sought to consolidate his future inheritance. Returning almost immediately to his campaign, Henry captured Sens only nine days after his marriage on 2 June 1420, pressing on towards Montereau-sur-Yonne, scene of Duke John's murder, before besieging the town of Melun between July and November, following which Henry entered Paris on 1 December 1420 as regent of France. He had achieved far more than he must have thought possible in 1417, partly through his own conquests and partly through the opportunities offered to him by the Armagnac and Burgundian conflict. He now felt secure enough in his position to return to England with his new bride in the early months of 1421.

The final campaign

Henry spent his time in England touring the country – showing the new queen to his subjects, visiting the major religious shrines and, above all, trying to drum up enthusiasm and support for his campaigns in France. Although the Treaty of Troyes had confirmed him as the legal heir to the throne of France,

The château of Alençon was constructed from the early 12th century, replacing an earlier structure dating from the time of the Conqueror. It was only finished in the early 15th century. The only surviving part of the castle from the period in question is the entrance portal, now the entrance to a prison. (Author's collection)

in practice the Dauphin and his Armagnac faction had control of the majority of France, and if Henry wanted to safeguard his new inheritance then he would have to fight for it.

He had not been long in England when he received disastrous news from his new realm. His brother, Thomas, Duke of Clarence, – who had been left in charge of Normandy in Henry's absence – had led a substantial force on a raid into the Armagnac-controlled territories of Maine and Anjou. Here he had encountered a major Franco-Scottish force at Baugé on 14 March 1421. Without waiting for his slow-moving archers to catch him up, Clarence launched a mounted charge at the Scottish troops, which, while initially successful, was later hampered by marshy ground while Scottish arrow fire cut down his men. The higher ranks of the army were particularly hard hit, with Thomas, Duke of Clarence, Sir Gilbert Umfraville and Sir John Grey all killed, while the Earl of Huntingdon was taken prisoner. The Earl of Salisbury succeeded in extracting the surviving English forces and retreated to the border of Normandy, which he proceeded to secure, and waited for the return of Henry to France.

Spurred on by the first military disaster of his campaigns, Henry redoubled his efforts to gain finance for more troops and supplies, and in May both parliament and the convocation of clergy granted him subsidies, while he also obtained a substantial amount through a loan from his uncle Henry Beaufort, Bishop of Winchester. At the same time he confiscated his stepmother Joan of Navarre's dowry after she was charged with witchcraft (a charge later dropped by Henry on his deathbed).

Henry used all this money to gather together a new army of 4,000–5,000 men and was back in Calais in June 1421, entering Paris on 4 July. Here he

Left: A medieval street in Alençon. The success of Henry's push southwards in 1417 was no doubt helped by the fact that the Duke of Alençon had perished in 1415 at the battle of Agincourt and the duchy was now in the hands of his infant son. The loss of a high proportion of the Norman aristocracy during the Agincourt campaign would ease Henry's conquests from 1417 to 1420. (Author's collection)

Right: A medieval arch in the town of Bellême in the Perche region of Normandy. This was probably the furthest point that Henry reached in his drive southwards in 1417 before turning back. (Author's collection)

In a break from standard medieval tradition, Henry carried on campaigning over the winter, besieging the town and castle of Falaise from December 1417 to February 1418. Following the submission of the garrison, Henry insisted that they repair the damage done by the English artillery to the fortifications of the town and castle before they were allowed to depart. (Author's collection)

replaced the Duke of Exeter as commander of the garrison with a Burgundian, thus removing a cause of civil unrest. Then, with his customary urgency and decisiveness, he relieved the siege of Chartres and besieged the Armagnac fortress of Dreux, which fell on 20 August. Henry then pushed on down towards the Loire Valley hoping to provoke the Dauphin into battle,

and even raided the outskirts of Orléans. But the Armagnacs would not come out of their defences, and Henry went eastwards, clearing fortifications on the Yonne and the Seine, before approaching the main target of his campaign, the town of Meaux some 48km (30 miles) to the east of Paris, on 6 October. This Armagnac stronghold had been launching raids to the very gates of Paris and had long been a thorn in the side of Henry's civil administration there. Again, Henry settled into the pattern of winter campaigning, dividing his army into four in order to cover all the approaches to the town, with each camp connected by trenches as at the siege of Rouen. An attempt by Guy de Nesle, Sire d'Offrément, to reinforce the garrison with 100 men-at-arms on 9 March 1422 failed and led to his capture, which so dispirited the defenders that they withdrew into the market, proposing to set fire to the old town. Henry found out about this move and managed to break into the old town

English campaigns in France, 1421–22

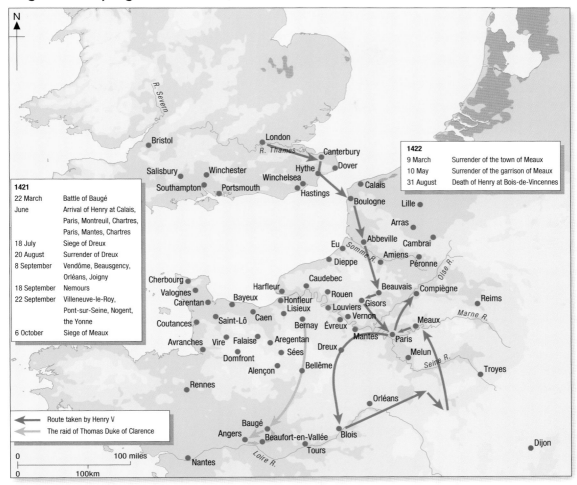

1421

22 March	Battle of Baugé
June	Arrival of Henry at Calais, Paris, Montreuil, Chartres, Paris, Mantes, Chartres
18 July	Siege of Dreux
20 August	Surrender of Dreux
8 September	Vendôme, Beausgency, Orléans, Joigny
18 September	Nemours
22 September	Villeneuve-le-Roy, Pont-sur-Seine, Nogent, the Yonne
6 October	Siege of Meaux

1422

9 March	Surrender of the town of Meaux
10 May	Surrender of the garrison of Meaux
31 August	Death of Henry at Bois-de-Vincennes

Route taken by Henry V
The raid of Thomas Duke of Clarence

0   100 miles
0   100km

before it could be fired, which left him only the market to deal with. Even so it held out for a further two months while Henry moved his artillery ever closer and closer. The inner fortifications finally surrendered on 10 May, with the Armagnac leaders being executed.

The siege of Meaux, as with many other of the sieges in Normandy, had seen outbreaks of disease amongst both the defenders and attacking forces, with dysentery being the principal culprit. On this occasion Henry also became ill, and, although he attempted to carry on with his campaigns, by July he could not mount a horse and was compelled to abandon his attempt to relieve Cosne-sur-Loire. He returned to the royal castle at Bois-de-Vincennes to the east of Paris where, having arranged the care of his kingdoms of France and England, as well as the upbringing of his infant son Henry (born on 6 December 1421), he died on the night of 31 August 1422. His body rested in state at Saint-Denis and Rouen before being taken across the channel on 31 October, being buried in Westminster Abbey on 7 November 1422.

Opposite: The capture of Pont-de-l'Arche by Henry V on 20 July 1418 gave him control of a major crossing over the Seine and meant that he was able to take his army into upper Normandy and towards the principal object of his campaign, Rouen. (Author's collection)

Top left: The Tour Jeanne d'Arc from the fortifications of Rouen. This tower is the only remaining structure of Rouen Castle, which was built by Philip Augustus from 1204 and demolished in the French Wars of Religion in 1591. Legend has it that Joan of Arc was held in this tower prior to her trial in 1430–31. (Author's collection)

Top Right: A medieval house in Rouen. The capital and most important town of the region, Rouen was the target of Henry's 1418 campaign, and fell after a six-month siege when the city's supplies had been long exhausted and no relief force was in sight. (Author's collection)

Middle: The château at Nogent-le-Retrou in the Perche region of Normandy. Constructed from the middle of the 11th century onwards, the castle formed part of the border region of Normandy and was captured by the English under Edward III in 1359. It is possible that Henry's forces reached this far in his campaigns of 1417–20, but it only finally fell into English hands following the battle of Verneuil in 1424. (Author's collection)

OPPOSING COMMANDERS

Henry's lengthy military career at home and in France saw him set against a range of opponents. From the Welsh rebellion that occupied his years as Prince of Wales, though the aristocratic revolts that bedevilled his father and spilled over into the early years of his reign to the royal family and great lords of France, who confronted him on the battlefield at Agincourt and vainly attempted to prevent his conquest of Normandy thereafter.

Owen Glendower

The leader of the Welsh revolt of 1400, Owen Glendower (or Owain Glyn Dwr) was born into an Anglo-Welsh gentry family at some point in the 1350s. He was descended on his mother's side from the welsh prince Llewellyn-ap-Graffyd who had fought against Edward I in the late 13th century, while on his father's side were the hereditary rulers of Powys Fadog. Owen was educated in the Anglo-Welsh tradition, comfortable in both languages and cultures; he even appears to have studied law at the Inns of Court in London for seven years.

He served under Richard II as a soldier in both France and Scotland, being knighted by Richard in 1387. He also saw service with Henry Bolingbroke, later Henry IV, at the battle of Radcot Bridge in 1387 against the interests of Richard II.

However, Welsh sympathy was largely with Richard in his dispute with Bolingbroke and the other Lords Appellant and it is against this background that he revolted against the Lancastrian monarch in September 1400, declaring himself the true Prince of Wales as the monarch was a usurper.

The immediate context to Owen's actions was a series of property disputes with his immediate neighbour, Lord Reginald de Grey of Ruthin, who was a

The seal of Owen Glendower, showing the Welsh lord sitting under a canopy and holding a sceptre. The only surviving copy of this seal was attached to the treaty between Glendower and Charles VI of France, signed in 1404, and the text around the outside most probably reads: 'OWEINUS DEI GRATIA PRINCEPS WALLIAE', 'Owen by the grace of god, Prince of Wales'. (Author's collection)

close intimate of Henry IV. Grey summoned Glendower late to a royal muster for the invasion of Scotland in 1400 and then accused him of treachery when he failed to appear. Glendower retaliated by sacking the town of Ruthin and plundering across the marcher lands and into Shropshire. When Henry IV returned from his Scottish expedition he found Wales on fire with rebellion and undertook a campaign to pacify the principality, outlawing Glendower and seizing his estates. However, this campaign failed to crush Glendower's revolt and he managed to capture Conwy Castle in April 1401 and win the battle of Mynydd Hyddgen in June 1401.

In the winter of 1401–02 he attacked Ruthin and managed to capture Grey himself; he then managed to defeat an English force under Sir Edmund Mortimer in the summer of 1402 at the battle of Pilleth, taking him captive as well. Although Grey was ransomed, Henry IV would not pay for Mortimer and he eventually sided with Glendower, marrying his daughter.

By 1403 the English presence was reduced to isolated fortresses, but they were beginning to fight back. Prince Henry managed to sack Glendower's properties at Sycharth and Glyndyvrdwy and his defeat at Carmathen on 12 July meant that he was unable to join up with the Percys at the battle of Shrewsbury, where their revolt was crushed.

Despite this setback, the fortunes of the Welsh revolt under Glendower were at their highest point in 1404 when, with active French support, Glendower was able to capture Harlech and Aberystwyth, holding court at the former and announcing a parliament and reform of the church and political system in Wales. The year 1405 was to see a further alliance between Glendower, Mortimer and the Earl of Northumberland, who are supposed to have intended to divide the country between the three of them in the 'triple indenture'. However, despite the presence of French forces in the country – who advanced as far as Worcester – 1405 was to see a number of setbacks for the revolt, with Prince Henry achieving successes in the field and Northumberland's conspiracy being exposed.

In June 1407 Prince Henry laid siege to Aberystwyth, using siege cannon against a fortress in England for the first time, and following its fall in the summer of 1408 the Welsh revolt became a protracted guerrilla war, with Glendower himself fading into the background. In February 1409 Harlech fell, along with many of Glendower's relatives, and Edmund Mortimer died, though Glendower himself remained at large and, according to the chronicler Adam of Usk, he died in 1415, possibly at the estates of his daughter and son-in-law in Herefordshire. Glendower has since become a symbol of Welsh national pride, particularly since the establishment of a separate Welsh parliament in 2000.

English magnates

The nature of Henry Bolingbroke's accession to the throne as Henry IV in September 1399 had caused a rift in the aristocratic community of England that would not be fully healed until the culmination of the Wars of the Roses in 1485. Those who supported the ousted king, Richard II, those who supported the superior claim to the throne of the houses of Mortimer and York, and even those who had supported the Lancastrian pretender, but felt they had not been rewarded enough for doing so, all at one stage or another set themselves up in opposition to Henry and his father.

Perhaps the most famous of these aristocratic adversaries was the Percy family of Northumberland. The Percys had been a major power in the north of England since they had gained their estates in the Norman Conquest. Richard II had created Henry Percy Earl of Northumberland in 1377, when he was also created Marshal of England. However, Northumberland had fallen out with Richard over his creation of Northumberland's great northern rivals the Neville family as Earls of Westmorland in 1397, and when Henry Bolingbroke returned to seek his lands in 1399 Northumberland was one of several powerful magnates who sided with him, though it is unclear if Northumberland expected Bolingbroke to take the throne.

Henry IV, as he was now known, had attained the throne based upon Richard II's failings and Henry's own legitimate claims, but right from the start his reign was plagued by political instability with the first signs of open aristocratic revolt coming in December 1399 when the Earls of Salisbury, Kent, Huntingdon and Rutland plotted to kill Henry at Windsor. Learning of the plot through Rutland, Henry managed to escape and the remaining earls were executed. This first rebellion provoked the death of Richard II, who up until that point had been kept alive, and he was certainly dead by 17 February.

On 14 September 1402 the Percys defeated a Scottish incursion at the battle of Homildon Hill. The force, commanded by the Earl of Northumberland and his son, Henry 'Hotspur' Percy, captured five Scottish earls and Henry IV demanded that they surrender their prisoners to the crown, thus depriving them of the potential ransom for them. Hotspur refused to hand over his most important captive, the Earl of Douglas, causing a breach between the Percys and the throne, a breach that had its beginnings in debts owed by Henry IV to the family, as well as his refusal to ransom Hotspur's brother-in-law, Sir Edmund Mortimer, from captivity in Wales.

This estrangement erupted into open revolt in 1403, when Hotspur, along with his uncle, the Earl of Worcester, sought to join forces with Owen Glendower and overthrow Henry IV in favour of the Earl of March. The issue was decided at the battle of Shrewsbury (pp.10–13) where Prince Henry won his spurs. Shakespeare has Prince Henry and Henry 'Hotspur' as equals, with Henry IV comparing his own son unfavourably with the young Percy:

In envy that my Lord Northumberland
Should be the father of so blest a son:

A son who is the theme of honour's tongue;
Amongst a grove, the very straightest plant,
Who is sweet Fortune's minion and her pride,
Whilst I, by looking on the praise of him,
See riot and dishonour stain the brow
Of my young Harry. O, that it could be proved
That some night-tripping fairy had exchanged
In cradle-clothes our children where they lay,
And called mine Percy, his Plantagenet:
Then would I have his Harry, and he mine.

1 Henry IV, I. i. 78–88

Shakespeare also has Prince Henry encountering Hotspur on the field of Shrewsbury before defeating him in single combat:

For worms brave Percy. Farwell, great heart!
Ill-weaved ambition, how much art though shrunk?

1 Henry IV, V. iii. 88–89

However, Henry and Hotspur were not contemporaries, with Henry being only a teenager at the battle of Shrewsbury and Hotspur in his late 30s or early 40s. It would also seem likely that if there was a chance that they had met in combat it would be mentioned in the various chronicles that deal with the battle.

Northumberland had been implicated in Hotspur's revolt, but the loss at Shrewsbury left him isolated and he made his peace with Henry IV at the expense of some of his lands and titles. However, the deaths of his son and brother ensured that he would not long remain docile and in 1405 he sided with Glendower and Mortimer once more, and supported a rebellion in the north in conjunction with Thomas Mowbray, Earl of Nottingham, Lord Bardolf and the Archbishop of York, Richard Scrope. Their conspiracy was thwarted through the efforts of the Earl of Westmorland, and Henry IV had Scrope and Mowbray executed, while Bardolf and Northumberland fled to Scotland. Northumberland had one final try at overthrowing the Lancastrian dynasty, venturing south in February 1408 with Bardolf once more. However, their force was decisively defeated at the battle of Bramham Moor on 19 February, with Northumberland being killed and Bardolf later dying of his wounds. This was the last major rebellion of Henry IV's reign, but the tension caused in aristocratic circles over the executions, notably that of Richard Scrope, would carry over into the reign of Henry V and culminate in the Southampton Plot of 1415.

On 31 July 1415, just prior to Henry's departure for France, the young Earl of March confessed his involvement in a threat to Henry's crown organized by Richard, Earl of Cambridge, Sir Thomas Grey, Lord Clifford and Lord Scrope – nephew of the executed Archbishop Scrope and one of Henry's closest advisors. The aim of the plot was to put the Earl of March on the throne in place of Henry, with support from the Scots and the Welsh and the Lollards under Sir John Oldcastle, who had rebelled the previous year. Though overly complicated and perhaps always doomed to failure, the revolt contained many of the names that had cropped up in the reign of Henry IV. Henry's reaction was swift, with Grey, Cambridge and Scrope all being arrested, sentenced and executed, in the one and only major aristocratic rebellion against his throne.

Indeed, Henry appears to have undertaken a programme of reconciliation towards those who had been attainted under his father. Henry Percy, son of Hotspur, who had fled to Scotland with Northumberland in 1405, was allowed to take his earldom in 1416, and Sir John Holland, whose father, the Earl of Huntingdon, had been executed for his involvement in an early revolt against Henry IV, became one of Henry's ablest lieutenants in the campaign and was restored to the earldom in 1416.

French lords

The natural leader of the French opposition to Henry's invasion of 1415 should have been the King of France, Charles VI. However, Charles was unsuitable for command in the field due to his mental state. Coming to the throne in 1380 at the age of 11, Charles was first struck by a fit of mental incapacity at the age of 21 and these recurred throughout his reign. His mental weakness led to a power struggle developing for control of the kingdom between the princes of the royal blood, notably Philip the Bold of Burgundy, the King's uncle, and Louis of Orléans, the King's brother. The death of Philip the Bold in 1404 saw his son John the Fearless take up the struggle, which culminated in the murder of Louis of Orléans in Paris in 1407, an act that led the two factions, the Burgundians and the Armagnacs – so called after the new duke, Charles of Orléans' father-in-law, Bernard VII, Count of Armagnac – to the brink of civil war. This left the French nobility split between two powerful factions and unable to unite even in the face of the external threat posed by Henry's invasion of 1415.

In the absence of the king, his heir, the Dauphin, might have been expected to take charge. However, the spectre of the capture of John II following the battle of Poitiers in 1356 haunted the French monarchy and the Dauphin, the 19-year-old Louis of Guienne, stayed with his father at Rouen.

The command of the French forces during the Agincourt campaign therefore devolved onto the other royal princes and dukes and those commanders appointed to the offices of Constable of France and Marshal of France. There was certainly a plethora of French aristocracy during the Agincourt campaign. Most senior was the 24-year-old Charles, Duke of Orléans, followed by the 33-year-old John, Duke of Bourbon, and the 30-year-old John,

An illustration from the *Chroniques* of Jean Froissart held in the Bibliothèque Nationale, Paris. To the left is shown Charles VI of France and to the right Henry V of England. By rights Charles VI should have been Henry's prime adversary during his campaigns in Normandy, but the French king's mental infirmity meant that it would have to be the Dauphin and the great lords of France that stood up to Henry. (akg-images/VISIOARS)

Marshal Boucicaut, Jean le Meingre, shown kneeling and praying at the bottom left of this illustration from a book of hours commissioned by him. His wife kneels opposite him. Boucicaut proved one of the more professional of the French commanders, but was restricted by the lack of unity within the French command. (Author's collection)

Duke of Alençon. None of these three had a great deal of military experience, certainly nothing to compare to Henry V, and much was expected of the Constable and Marshal of France.

The Constable was Charles d'Albret, who had served in the role from 1402 to 1411 before being dismissed by the Burgundian faction. The Armagnac rise to power saw him restored to his role in 1413 and he was a professional soldier of long standing. The Marshal was an even more famous warrior, Jean le Meingre. Known as Boucicaut, his father had also been Marshal and he served at the battle of Roosebeke of 1382 where he was knighted. He then fought with the Teutonic Order in Livonia and Prussia throughout the 1380s and 90s, before taking part in the Franco-Hungarian crusade against the Ottomans that came to grief at the battle of Nicopolis in 1396 at the hands of the Ottoman sultan Bayezid. Boucicaut was captured here and spent time at the Ottoman capital Bursa before being ransomed. He returned to Constantinople in 1399 to defend Genoese interests there. In addition to his military exploits he had also founded a chivalric order in 1399, the Emprise de l'Escu vert à la Dame Blanche, and was widely respected throughout both armies.

Of these senior French commanders, d'Albret fell on the battlefield of Agincourt as did Alençon. Boucicaut, Orléans and Bourbon became prisoners of the English, destined to spend a long time in captivity. Bourbon and Boucicaut both died in captivity, the former at Bolingbroke in 1434, the latter in Yorkshire in 1421. Charles, Duke of Orléans, would return to France, but not until 1440, apparently speaking English rather better than his native French.

Following the death or capture of so many of France's leaders at the battle of Agincourt, a whole new generation of commanders was required to try and stem Henry's subsequent conquest of Normandy, of which the most notable was the new Dauphin of France following the deaths of both Louis of Guienne in 1415 and his successor, John, Duke of Touraine, – Charles, Count of Ponthieu. Charles was unable to prevent Henry's conquests of 1417–19, and his acquiescence in the murder of John the Fearless of Burgundy in 1419 drove the Burgundian faction into the hands of the English and nearly lost him his crown, disinherited as he was by the Treaty of Troyes in 1420. However, following the death of both Henry V and his father, and the putative accession to the French throne of the young Henry VI, Charles claimed the throne as Charles VII and, assisted by Joan of Arc, was crowned in Reims in July 1429. By the end of his reign Charles had succeeded in recapturing all of the lands lost to the English with the exception of the immediate area around Calais.

WHEN WAR IS DONE

Hung be the heavens with black: yield, day, to night!
Comets, importing change of times and states,
Brandish your crystal tresses in the sky,
And with them scourge the bad revolting stars
That have consented unto Henry's death:
King Henry the Fifth, too famous to live long:
England ne'er lost a king of so much worth.

1 Henry VI, I. i. 1–7

So Shakespeare has John, Duke of Bedford, Henry's younger brother, lamenting at the beginning of his play *Henry VI, Part I*. The Duke of Bedford was to play a central role in the organization and defence of the English kingdom of France created by Henry's conquests and now inherited by his son, the new Henry VI. Henry V had given much thought to the disposition of his conquests as well as his soul in his final days, and the writer of the *The First English Life of Henry V* describes the careful manner in which he arranged for the governance of his kingdom:

> The Kings disease dayly increased, vntill that most Christian Kinge yealded his soule to God, departed this life in the Castell of that is called Bois de Vistenne [Bois-de-Vincennes], not farr from Parris; where at that time was present Kinge Charles and the two Queenes. But tofore his death this most prudent Kinge in his Testament disposed the care and garde of the younge Prince, his sonn, and the defence of the Realme of Englande, to his most deere brother, Humphrie, Duke of Glocester… the custody of the bodie of the younge Prince the Kinge committed to his vnckle the Duke of Excester, to endoctrine him in all good manners. And the reuenews of the Dutchie of Normandie the Kinge bequeathe to his right puissant brother John, Duke of Bedforde, for the gouernance and defence of the same Dutchie and of the Realme of Fraunce.

In the event, the parliament of December 1422 preferred to appoint Bedford as 'protector, defender and chief councillor of England', with Humphrey, Duke of Gloucester, only acting in his stead when he was out of the country fulfilling his role in France. In addition to this, parliament was unwilling to accept one individual as regent, appointing a council of 16 instead to govern the country. This caused a degree of inter-magnate rivalry and strife, particularly between Gloucester and his uncle, Henry Beaufort,

Troyes Cathedral provided the backdrop for the signing of the Treaty of Troyes on the high altar on 21 May 1420, following which Henry and Katherine were betrothed in the same church. This was the document that really established the Lancastrian kingdom of France inherited by Henry VI in 1422. (Author's collection)

An illustration from a 15th-century French manuscript stored in the Bibliothèque Nationale, Paris (Ms. français 2678, fol.35 v. Paris), showing the signing of the Treaty of Troyes on 21 May 1420. Henry V is shown to the left with Philip of Burgundy to the right. Philip's abandonment of his English alliance and reconciliation with Charles VII in 1435 proved the decisive blow for English hopes in France. (akg-images/VISIOARS)

Bishop of Winchester and, from 1426, Cardinal. The split in the council developed into a pro-war party – led by Gloucester – and those who sought a more conciliatory line – led by Beaufort.

In France matters were simpler, particularly when Charles VI died only seven weeks after Henry on 21 October 1422. This left John, Duke of Bedford, as regent for Henry VI in France and he carried out his duties with great ability, securing the Anglo-Burgundian alliance through his marriage to Anne of Burgundy in June 1423. He won battlefield victories over Anglo-Scots forces at Cravant in 1423 and Verneuil in 1424 that opened the way for further English conquests and advances into Maine and down to the Loire, leading to the siege of Orléans in October 1428. However, the French, inspired by Joan of Arc, raised the siege of Orléans in 1429 and defeated the English in battle at Patay in the same year, opening up the road to Reims for Joan and the Dauphin, with him being crowned Charles VII there on 17 July 1429. This caused a crisis in the English possessions in France with Paris itself threatened. Although Bedford managed to stabilize the situation, momentum had swung back to the French and, following Bedford's death in 1435, the Duke of Burgundy split with the English and allied himself to Charles VII through the Treaty of Arras, irrevocably shifting the balance of military power against the English forces, with Paris falling in 1436. Henry VI's assumption of full power did little to halt this trend, and by 1440 Harfleur had been reconquered by the French before a truce was agreed in May 1444. This lasted for five years until Charles VII, having built up his forces, declared war on 17 July 1449. In a rapid campaign he swept up the remaining English positions in Normandy, with Rouen falling on 29 October and the English decisively defeated at Formigny on 15 April 1450; Cherbourg, the last English-held place in Normandy, finally surrendered on 12 August. Charles VII then turned to Gascony and cleared the English from their last major possession in France, with Bordeaux finally falling on 19 October 1453.

The series of defeats in Normandy and Gascony, combined with Henry VI's vacillating leadership, led to a series of increasingly bitter disputes between his magnates, with Edward, Duke of York, leading the calls for reform. These aristocratic disputes would break out into the Wars of the Roses that would ultimately see the downfall of the Lancastrian kingdom of France as well as England.

So Henry V's achievements did not prove to be particularly long lasting, but his battlefield victory at Agincourt was stunning, and his campaign to reduce the fortifications of Normandy and beyond was impressive in its planning, organization and intensity, a fact recognized by French commentators as well as more biased English ones. He benefited enormously in both campaigns from a fatal lack of unity on the French side caused by the state of near civil war that existed between the Armagnac and Burgundian factions and the mental incapacity of Charles VI. So much of the solidity of Henry's conquests was based upon his reputation and authority and, following his early death and the reconciliation between Burgundy and the Crown, there was little that the English could do to preserve their territories in France.

INSIDE THE MIND

Henry V has been heralded by many as the perfect medieval king, lauded by the historian K. B. MacFarlane as 'the greatest man that ever ruled England', while contemporary commentators, both English and French, praised his abilities and achievements. These fitted neatly into the medieval paradigm of kingship, based around the ideal king being militarily brave and successful, a defender of the faith and Christian orthodoxy and an impartial upholder of law and order.

In many ways Henry certainly did fill these criteria. That he was personally brave is undoubted – his severe wounding in the face at Shrewsbury is an early example of this, with Henry returning to the battle and only seeking medical aid once the victory was won. During the Agincourt campaign he exposed himself to danger at the siege of Harfleur and then fought in the front line of men-at-arms at the battle of Agincourt itself. Various chronicles have him

The saddle of Henry V from his tomb in Westminster Abbey. It would have originally been covered in blue velvet decorated with fleurs-de-lys. (Copyright Dean and Chapter of Westminster)

standing over the body of his brother, Humphrey, Duke of Gloucester, fighting off the French, while other sources relate how 18 squires of the Sire de Croy attempted to kill him, with one managing to strike one of the fleurets off his crown before they were all killed (other sources attribute this to the Duke of Alençon). The chronicler of St Albans, Thomas Walsingham, says of Henry at the battle: 'He both inflicted and received cruel wounds, offering an example in his own person to his men by his bravery in scattering the opposing battle lines with a battle axe', while Tito Livio says he fought 'like an unvanquished lion' and the *Gesta Henrici Quinti* relates how 'Nor do our older men remember any prince having commanded his people on the march with more effort, bravery or consideration, or having, with his own hand, performed greater feats of strength in the field.' This impression of personal bravery is confirmed in the later campaigns when he exposed himself to danger at various sieges, including fighting in the mines beneath the town of Melun during the siege of 1420.

However, his military achievements, particularly in the campaigns from 1417 to 1420, were not based so much upon his personal reputation for bravery, but upon his organizational and logistic skills in keeping a well-supplied army in the field year round, enabling him to take town after town, fortress after fortress, constantly keeping his enemies under pressure and creating a momentum behind his conquests that led to some towns and fortifications capitulating merely at the arrival of his army. His success in these various campaigns and sieges merely confirmed in his eyes, and many of his contemporaries, that he and his cause were favoured by God.

His personal religious beliefs appear to have been orthodox and deeply held. Even before his accession to the throne he was involved in the suppression of the Lollard heresy, being present at the burning of John Badby in 1409 and supporting Archbishop Thomas Arundel's purge of Lollards from Oxford University in 1411. After his accession he himself had to deal with the Lollard-inspired Oldcastle Revolt in 1414, though it is possible that contemporary chroniclers have over-emphasized the seriousness of this rebellion.

Despite the dissolute reputation of the 'Hal' of Shakespeare's *Henry IV, Part I* and *Henry IV, Part II*, there is little evidence of any disorder in his personal life prior to his gaining the throne, and his personal religious fervour is further attested to by his interest in and patronage of the austere Carthusian Order. He was the last English king to found new religious houses, and the Carthusian house at Sheen and Brigittine house at Syon, both founded in 1415, were the last major foundations prior to the Reformation.

His interest in law and order and impartial justice, key aspects of medieval kingship, also appear to have been sincerely held and to have applied both in England and France. Right at the beginning of his reign he offered a general pardon for offences committed in his father's reign, a policy that was particularly effective in Wales following the collapse of the Glendower revolt. He was also particularly conciliatory to the descendants of those who had fallen foul of his father during the turbulent years of the early 15th century, restoring men such as John Holland – the future Earl of Huntingdon – to his estates, negotiating with the son of Henry Hotspur for his return from Scotland and appointing Lord Mowbray to his hereditary title of Earl Marshal. Although conciliatory at times, he could also be vindictive, with Henry, Lord Scrope, being executed in disgrace for a flimsy involvement in the Southampton Plot while Henry Beaufort's appointment as Cardinal and papal legate in 1417 saw him lose Henry's favour until he had refused the honours and offered Henry some £22,000 in loans.

Henry also made concrete efforts to improve the law-and-order situation throughout his kingdom, instigating special commissions of the King's Bench in an effort to put down disorder in Staffordshire and Shropshire, and he was not afraid to fine one of his most important supporters, Thomas, Earl of Arundel, in the process. There is some evidence that the relatively peaceful state of England during his reign, so unusual in the 15th century, began to break down during the latter years of his reign while he was absent in France. In France itself he issued famous ordinances regulating the behaviour of his men prior to his campaigns in both 1415 and 1417, famously hanging one of his army for stealing a pyx from a church on the march from Harfleur to Agincourt.

However, though all sides agreed that Henry could exercise mercy as befitted a Christian king of the period, he was also ruthless in his campaigning and capable of acts of brutality. The slaughter of the prisoners in the confused situation towards the end of the battle of Agincourt may not in the medieval context have been what we today would term a 'war crime', and it may certainly have been militarily justifiable at the time, but it certainly did not fit the ideal of a Christian king. Following the siege of Meaux he had a trumpeter who had insulted him executed, while at the earlier siege of Melun

Reims Cathedral, the traditional site for the coronation of kings of France. Although John, Duke of Bedford, had hoped to have the young Henry VI crowned here, the Dauphin and Joan of Arc beat him to it, entering Reims on 16 July 1429 and he was crowned Charles VII, king of France, on the 17th. (Author's collection)

he had hanged 20 Scots on the somewhat dubious basis that their imprisoned king (in Henry's custody) had ordered them not to fight, and at the siege of Louviers in 1418 he hanged eight gunners who had come near to killing him during the siege.

A LIFE IN WORDS

Henry V was well aware of the power of the written word and many of the earliest sources for his campaigns and reign were written while he was still alive. The *Gesta Henrici Quinti*, widely acknowledged as the most reliable English source for the Agincourt campaign, was written by an anonymous chaplain in the royal service and was probably finished in either 1416 or 1417. The impression of Henry as a servant of God in both his suppression of the Lollards and defeat of the French at Agincourt is perhaps unsurprising given the author's royal connections. The only other strictly contemporary work is the *Liber Metricus* of Thomas Elmham, and this work follows a similar line to the *Gesta*. The *Vita Henrici Quinti* by Tito Livio was written in the 1430s after Henry's death, though there is a strong suspicion that it was commissioned by Henry's brother, Humphrey, Duke of Gloucester, in an effort to emphasize the Duke's close personal relationship to Henry and thus advance his political position.

Thomas Hoccleve (*c.*1368–1426) presenting a copy of his *De Regimine Principum* (*Regiment of Princes*) to Prince Henry in around 1413. Even before his accession to the throne Henry was well aware of the power of the written word and would always seek to win the propaganda war. This illumination is from a manuscript (Ms. Arundel 38, fol. 37) held in the British Library, London. (akg-images/ British Library)

The French sources might be expected to be more negative towards Henry, yet although they are mostly negative about the English in general and the English presence in France specifically, they generally speak highly of Henry's abilities as a medieval king and military leader, with the monk of Saint-Denis stating that 'No prince in his time appeared more capable to subdue and conquer a country, by the wisdom of his government, by his prudence and by the other qualities with which he was endowed', while Jean de Waurin, the Burgundian chronicler, describes him as 'a most clever man and expert in everything he undertook'.

It is with the Tudors that Henry's reputation began to be set in stone. The nature of the Tudors' accession to the throne of England meant that they were keen to emphasize the restorative nature of their rule by denigrating their 15th-century predecessors, so Henry IV is portrayed as a usurper, Henry VI as weak and vacillating and Richard III as the cruel hunchback of popular imagination. The one exception to this list of villains is Henry V, whose reputation is enhanced throughout the period for his supposed embodiment of chivalric ideals and, perhaps more importantly, his victories over the French. The early years of the reign of Henry VIII saw the publication of *The First English Life of Henry V*, which is largely based upon the earlier work of Tito Livio. It was written in 1513 partly to inspire Henry VIII in his campaigns against France and uses Henry V as an example for the 16th-century Henry to follow. This idea of Henry as an exemplar of medieval kingship carried on into the Elizabethan period, and runs through the works of writers such as Richard Grafton and is emphasized in one of the most famous works of history of the period, *Holinshed's Chronicles of England, Scotland and Ireland*, published in 1586–87. Compiled by Raphael Holinshed and others, this work synthesized a range of 15th- and 16th-century sources and provided a good source of material for the many dramatists of the period, including William Shakespeare.

Shakespeare was not the first playwright to take Henry V as his theme. *The Famous Victories of Henry V: Containing the Honourable Battle of Agincourt* by an unknown author was used by Shakespeare, along with Holinshed and other sources, when he came to writing his cycle of history plays that has been so influential in preserving an image of Henry throughout the years. Shakespeare's Henry appears in three plays: *Henry IV, Part I, Henry IV, Part II* and *Henry V*. The Henry, or Hal, of the first two plays is a wastrel prince engaged in dissolute activity with his drinking companions, while at the same time supporting his father at the battle of Shrewsbury when he is in time of need. The Henry of *Henry V* is the familiar charismatic warrior king, encouraging his troops with 'a little touch of Harry in the night' and leading them to victory on St Crispin's Day before wooing the French princess Katherine. Though Shakespeare paints a largely heroic picture of Henry, he does have him giving the order to kill the prisoners at Agincourt and foreshadows the temporary nature of his achievements:

> Henry the Sixth, in infant bands crowned King
> Of France and England, did this king succeed.
> Whose state so many had the managing,
> That they lost France and made his England
>   bleed,

Henry V, Ep. 9–12

This portrait (oil on canvas) of William Shakespeare (1564–1616) was painted between 1600 and 1610 and is attributed to John Taylor. It is popularly known as the Chandos Portrait, after one of its owners, and was the first bequest to the National Portrait Gallery on its foundation in 1856. (National Portrait Gallery, London, UK/The Bridgeman Art Library)

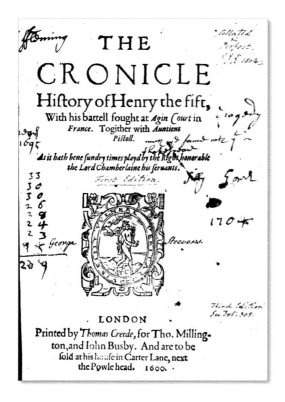

The title page of the first quarto edition of Shakespeare's Henry V, published in 1600. The play is thought to have first been performed at the Globe theatre between February and September 1599. (Author's collection)

It is this image of Henry as military hero that has remained through to the 20th century, reintroduced in the age of film through the performances and direction of Laurence Olivier in his 1944 version and Kenneth Branagh in 1989. Olivier's version, coming at the height of World War II, is perhaps understandably propagandist, down to its dedication 'To the commandos and airborne troops of Great Britain', while Branagh's film is much grittier in its portrayal of the battle scenes in particular.

Modern academic tradition has a much more nuanced view of Henry and his achievements, though still influenced by the work of the noted 20th-century medievalist K. B. MacFarlane, who considered Henry the greatest man to have ruled England. The late 20th century and early 21st century has seen something of an explosion of works on the subject, helped no end by the translation of sources of the battle published by Anne Curry in 2000, while recent work on the financial records of both sides has shed new light on the numbers involved in both the Agincourt campaign and the foundation of Lancastrian Normandy.

FURTHER READING

In recent years there has been a proliferation of material on both Henry V and the Lancastrian kingdom of France, with recent works by Juliet Barker being popular, well written and scholarly. Ian Mortimer's just published day-by-day account of the year 1415 puts much of the run up to the battle of Agincourt within its European context and is useful for the insights it provides in that direction.

Anne Curry's work on Henry V and the Hundred Years War has proved particularly valuable, in particular her edited sources for the battle, while her *Agincourt: A New History* dramatically revises the numbers involved in the battle based upon her use of financial records from both the English and French sides; mention must also be made of the online database developed by Anne Curry amongst others listing English soldiers involved in the Hundred Years War: http://www.icmacentre.ac.uk/soldier/database/.

Printed primary material

Cole, Charles Augustus, *Memorials of Henry the Fifth, King of England* Longman, Brown, Green, Longmans, and Roberts: London, 1858

Curry, Anne (ed.), *The battle of Agincourt: Sources and Interpretations* Boydell Press: Woodbridge, 2000

Given-Wilson, C. (ed.), *The Chronicle of Adam Usk, 1377–1421* Clarendon Press: Oxford, 1997

Kingsford, C. L. (ed.), *The first English life of king Henry the fifth ... by an anonymous author known commonly as the translator of Livius* Oxford, 1911

Taylor, Frank, and Roskell, John S. (eds.), *Gesta Henrici Quinti* Clarendon Press: Oxford, 1975

Secondary material

Allmand, C. T., *Henry V,* Methuen: London, 1992

Barker, Juliet, *Agincourt: the King, the Campaign, the Battle* Little, Brown: London, 2005

——, *Conquest: the English Kingdom of France, 1417–1450* Little, Brown: London, 2009

Bennett, Matthew, Campaign 9: *Agincourt 1415* Osprey Publishing Ltd: Oxford, 1991

Curry, Anne (ed.), *Agincourt, 1415: Henry V, Sir Thomas Erpingham and the Triumph of the English Archers* Tempus: Stroud, 2005

Curry, Anne, *Agincourt: A New History* Tempus: Stroud, 2005

Curry, Anne, and Hughes, Michael, (eds.) *Arms, Armies and Fortifications in the Hundred Years War* Boydell Press: Woodbridge, 1994

——, *The Hundred Years' War, 1337–1457* Osprey Publishing Ltd: Oxford, 2002

Dockray, Keith, *Warrior king: the Life of Henry V* Tempus: Stroud, 2007

Hardy, Robert, *Longbow: a Social and Military History* Patrick Stephens: Sparkford, 1992

Jones, Michael K., *Agincourt 1415* Pen & Sword: Barnsley, 2005

Keen, M. H., *England in the Later Middle Ages: a Political History* Methuen: London, 1973

——, *Medieval Warfare: a History* Oxford University Press: Oxford, 1999

Knight, Paul, *Henry V and the Conquest of France 1416–53* Osprey Publishing Ltd: Oxford, 1998

McFarlane, K. B., *Lancastrian Kings and Lollard Knights* Clarendon Press: Oxford, 1972

Mortimer, Ian, *The fears of Henry IV: the Life of England's Self-Made King* Jonathan Cape: London, 2007

——, *1415: Henry V's Year of Glory* The Bodley Head: London, 2009

Rothero, Christopher, Men-at-Arms 113: *The Armies of Agincourt* Osprey Publishing Ltd: Oxford, 1981

Seward, Desmond, *Henry V as Warlord* Sidgwick & Jackson: London, 1987

Shakespeare, William, *Complete Works* Macmillan: Basingstoke, 2007

INDEX

References to illustrations are shown in **bold**. Plates are prefixed pl, with captions on the page in brackets.